MID-LIFE
DIVORCE
COUNSELING

Edited by Lita Linzer Schwartz

AMERICAN
COUNSELING
ASSOCIATION

■ ■ ■
THE FAMILY PSYCHOLOGY AND COUNSELING SERIES
Jon Carlson, Editor

Mid-Life Divorce Counseling

10 9 8 7 6 5 4 3 2 1

American Counseling Association
5999 Stevenson Avenue
Alexandria, VA 22304

Director of Communications
Jennifer L. Sacks

Acquisitions and Development Editor
Carolyn Baker

Production/Design Manager
Michael Comlish

Copyeditor
Heather Jefferson

Cover design by Martha Woolsey

Library of Congress Cataloging-in-Publication Data

Mid-life divorce counseling / edited by Lita Linzer Schwartz.
    p. cm.—(The Family psychology and counseling series)
Includes bibliographical references.
ISBN 1-55620-131-1
    1. Divorce counseling—United States. 2. Middle aged persons—Counseling of—United States. 3. Midlife crisis—United States.
I. Schwartz, Lita Linzer. II. Series.
HQ834.M53 1994   93-36923
362.82′86—dc20   CIP

The Family Psychology and Counseling Series

Mid-Life Divorce Counseling
Lita Linzer Schwartz, Ph.D.

Transitioning from Individual to Family Counseling
Charles Huber, Ph.D.

In Preparation

Assessment and Diagnosis of Step-Families
Debra Huntley, Ph.D.

Counseling Aging Parents and Their Families
Irene Deitch, Ph.D.

Counseling Families with Chronic Illness
Susan McDaniel, Ph.D.

Counseling Substance Abusers and Their Families
Judith Lewis, Ph.D.

■ ■ ■
THE FAMILY PSYCHOLOGY AND COUNSELING SERIES

Table of Contents

PART II. COMMON THERAPEUTIC TECHNIQUES

PART III. LEGAL ISSUES IN MID-LIFE DIVORCE

Foreword

Family and couple is a rapidly growing specialty area of counseling and psychology. Ideas, techniques, and theories are being generated in a variety of areas at an unprecedented rate. Most seemingly important areas are receiving some attention; however, there are many areas that need a more detailed treatment. A monograph is a book that has one specific focus or topic. *The Family Psychology and Counseling Series* provides a vehicle for professionals to address the important issues of today in depth. All topics have been selected through a polling of professionals. The editors are carefully appointed, and all manuscripts, although invited, are peer reviewed. The emphasis is on practice and application. All procedures must be based on sound empirical research. However, the focus is on the application of the research, rather than how the research was conducted.

The Family Psychology and Counseling Series highlights key challenges facing professionals today, bringing together theoreticians and practitioners to present the best knowledge and approaches available. By refocusing and integrating our thinking and developing new intervention skills, counselors can help people develop marriages and families that are responsive to the many challenges of today. The future of marital and family counseling/ psychology lies in the deemphasis of competing therapies and the development of a tested set of broadly accepted principles of systemic prevention that have specific components and therapeutic behaviors. This is the time for integration, evaluation, and digestion, rather than bold new paradigms. *The Family Psychology and Counseling Series* is the place for this to occur.

—*Jon Carlson, PsyD, EdD*

From the Series Editor

When the topic of mid-life divorce was initially suggested, I must admit that I was somewhat skeptical. However, as time passed, I began noticing mid-life issues and themes of my own as well as those of my friends and clients. Many of us are in our 40s and 50s. I began to notice couples in dysfunctional marriages who were divorcing or on the brink of separating, couples whose marriages ended as children grew up and left home, and couples whose marriages were destabilized by either career setbacks, career advances, or serious illness. Many marriages were being devastated by affairs and by partners changing their roles, identities, and even their values. One colleague indicated if identity crises strike us at adolescence, they also tend to strike marriages at mid-life and probably for a good reason. The family focus is shifting to a couple focus, but we're hardly the same couple we were 20 years ago. Both partners have changed, and they are no longer defining themselves through their marriage in terms of their responsibilities to others. The shift has moved from "what am I *supposed* to do or be?" to "what or who do I *want* to do or be?"

Mid-life seems to be a time for role swapping as men become more feminine and women become more masculine. The roles and subsequent rules of living together have changed markedly. This is a natural time for conflict. Few couples know how to deal effectively with conflict and therefore repair or healing does not occur, leaving the couple unable to move beyond the conflict. At mid-life, almost every marriage undergoes a crisis, and most people are looking for a way to get through this crisis, not out of the marriage. Unfortunately, divorce does occur. Statistics show three dramatic divorce peaks: between 2 to 4 years, 15 to 18 years, and 25 to 28 years of marriage.

Divorce in mid-life seems to result from a failure to negotiate new issues, rather than from some long-standing incompatibility. Renewing a marriage takes energy, desire, and dedication that a couple is unlikely to have available when their resources are used in conflict. The marriages that don't survive seem to lack commitment, sexual and/or emotional chemistry, areas of mutual enjoyment, or mutual respect.

Lita Linzer Schwartz and her colleagues have brought together the most comprehensive study on mid-life divorce to date. The chapters clearly present this treatment population and the challenges they present to the practicing counselor or psychologist.

—Jon Carlson, PsyD, EdD
Series Editor

Preface

"I arose this morning and said to myself, 'Today is the beginning of my new life. Yesterday I was married; today count me among the divorced.' " Not everyone suddenly separated or divorced thinks or says this consciously, but the feeling is there. If the new life is confronted when one is in the 40s, 50s, or 60s, after a marriage of 20 years or more, questions arise that differ from those faced by younger divorced people. Typically, personality traits and behaviors are well established; one has become accustomed to a particular life-style (precrisis); and the care of minor children is less often an issue.

Mid-life divorce, in contrast with divorce in early marriage, often occurs in families that are regarded as having good relationships by one or both marital partners and by most outsiders. There are challenges to marriage at this point, however: personal growth, the need to revise expectations, mutual needs for emotional support in the face of physical and familial transitions, renewal of romance and sexual pleasure, and exploration of new directions (Catron, 1990). The initiation of a separation or divorce at this point may be an attempt to solve some of these problems on a personal level for one of the partners or on an interpersonal level regarding the dyadic relationship. According to Iwanir and Ayal (1991), "The most likely causes are rigidity in communication patterns, an inadequately developed mechanism for coping with conflicts and making decisions, and an inflexible definition of their boundaries and hierarchical relationships" (p. 611). Marital and divorce counseling both focus on remediating these difficulties.

There are a number of factors that bear on the person who experiences a mid-life divorce (Schwartz, 1989). Age, for the purposes of this discussion, includes individuals in the 40–60 age range. (Those at the upper end of the range, particularly if they are active and/or employed, tend to view themselves as middle-aged people rather than as senior citizens.) Gender, as will be apparent in a number of the chapters, has a differential impact on the life issues to be confronted and on the individual's long-term adjustment. Other aspects of life, moreover, enter the picture as they might not at a younger age: health (encompassing care as well as medical expense coverage), employability, maintenance of one's life-style, and the nature and quality of opportunities for social life, among others.

Let us put today's mid-life generation into a historical context, the better to examine its complexities. The principals were born into a world quite different from today's, the late 1920s to perhaps the mid-1940s, and married in the post-World War II era when raising a family was a woman's most important and, perhaps, only job. Higher education was not common prior to the war, especially for females, nor were professional or executive careers perceived as appropriate for females, especially those who were married.

Middle-class women of this cohort might have worked for compensation before marriage, but rarely afterward. Their identities were in terms of being "Joe's wife" and "Betty's and Billy's mother." Their husbands were the wage earners with minimal roles in the home. Most studies of children in the period, in fact, did not even question what impact men might have as fathers, whereas they roundly condemned working mothers. Among those less affluent, women did work outside the home, often alongside their husbands in the small family business or in low-paying, low-status jobs. As a few of the authors in this book note, this creates a different situation for them at a time of mid-life divorce.

Depending on whether the authors are addressing the lower end of the mid-life age range or the upper end, and also depending on the length of the marriage, custody arrangements and grandparent visiting rights may or may not be addressed. These questions tend to be somewhat less involved in mid-life divorce as any children are likely to be adolescents or young adults, and therefore have, or should have, more input about their postdivorce lives than is true for younger children. One critical issue for them, if still adolescents, revolves around who will pay for higher education.

For all of those divorcing, the amount of forewarning of the impending change in status makes a difference in the time needed to adjust. Whichever spouse is the abandoned one tends to be the one less prepared and therefore the one who has the greater adjustment to make. The availability of a support network—children, extended family, and/or friends—may be a critical factor in the eventual recovery for the abandoned spouse. The initiator, on the other hand, rarely suffers the loss of self-esteem that the abandoned one does and may be looking forward to a new life-style and/or a new spouse. As the clinicians here indicate, much of the client's "recovery" depends also on the individual's precrisis personal characteristics, locus of control, and powers of resilience.

In focusing on divorce at mid-life, several different perspectives are represented here. Several clinicians discuss the problems their clients have brought to them and the ways in which divorcing clients can be helped to rebound; two researchers focus on the issues of mental and physical health, and a judge shares his views of the legal wrangles brought to his court.

Carol Philpot, who practices in Florida, focuses on the motives for initiating divorce proceedings, considering the sociological as well as the therapeutic implications for those involved. She examines the "stations" of divorce (after Bohannon, 1970), but with some different emphases, especially the impact of gender socialization.

It should be noted that there are other theories of the stages of divorce, notably those offered by Froiland and Hozeman (1975), Kessler (1975), and Wiseman (1975). These theoretical contexts and others are discussed and presented in tabular form by Raschke (1987).

Diana and Sam Kirschner were asked to do their chapter jointly because they have been in practice together in Pennsylvania for many years. The result of their efforts speaks to the masculine mid-life crisis, which may or may not lead to divorce, so they offer a viewpoint that is often neglected.

To provide other perspectives on mid-life divorce, Charles Hennon and Timothy Brubaker were invited to present the fruits of their research in the area of health under these circumstances. Their chapter brings the research and statistical perspective to the fore in a way that specifics and generalizations from case histories cannot. Using statistical data that extend over decades, they suggest changes over time that affect present views of mid-life divorce and that may have impact on those who divorce at mid-life in the future.

Florence Kaslow, a leading marriage and family therapist who practices in southern Florida, and a prolific author in this field, has chosen to explore the dynamics of a single case. Throughout the discussion of this case, she demonstrates the different stages the participants go through and the several realms of their lives on which the divorce has impact. This is shown clearly in her diaclectic model.

Lita Schwartz's contributions focus on cases that stress the unique character of the impact of divorce on individuals. The first chapter, a brief interview with Sidney Segal, also provides a masculine perspective. In addition to presenting cases in which the principals appear to have gone to extremes in their efforts to dissolve a marriage, he offers constructive suggestions for those mid-life (and other) clients who would truly prefer to save their marriages. In her second chapter, the variations on the theme are all female.

Bruce Fisher, a Colorado practitioner, offers a perspective focused on rebuilding one's life after a significant part of it has ended, which is, after all, the goal for most clients. He also introduces his divorce class, which suggests a unique approach that others might like to emulate.

Walter Schackman was asked to share a judicial view. Justice Schackman's remarks, in fact, were chosen to appear here as they reflect a necessarily more objective experience than that of clinicians and bring a legal perspective to the mid-life divorce controversies. Not only does he have to listen to the anger, pain, and arguments, as clinicians do, but he then has to decide between the parties' claims in a way that clinicians do not. His thoughts set the stage, as it were, for the more individual situations discussed by those in private practice.

Peter Rogers and Martina Reaves discuss mediation and the mid-life divorce from the perspectives of counseling and the law. Mid-life divorce involves ending both a personal relationship and a long-term business relationship. Mediation can be used effectively by divorcing partners to dissolve their relationship and empower them to make decisions about their futures.

Although many of the authors work in academia as well as in private practice, they were urged to write, if possible, in a nonpedantic style ... more as if they were talking to the reader or to a group. They were also encouraged to take a practical rather than an abstract or theoretical perspective, as this volume focuses on applications more than theories. I hope you will agree that they have succeeded in their efforts.

References

Bohannon, P. (1970). The six stations of divorce. In P. Bohannon (Ed.), *Divorce and after: An analysis of the emotional and social problems of divorce* (pp. 29–55). New York, NY: Doubleday.

Catron, S.S. (1990). *Mid-life marriage: Choices and chances for change.* Winston-Salem, NC: The Association for Couples in Marriage Enrichment.

Froiland, D.J., & Hozeman, T.L. (1975). Counseling for constructive divorce. *Personnel and Guidance Journal, 55*, 525–529.

Iwanir, S., & Ayal, H. (1991). Midlife divorce initiation: From crisis to developmental transition. *Contemporary Family Therapy, 13*, 609–623.

Kessler, S. (1975). *The American way of divorce: Prescriptions for change.* Chicago, IL: Nelson-Hall.

Raschke, H.J. (1987). Divorce. In M.B. Sussman & S.K. Steinmetz (Eds.), *Handbook of marriage and the family.* New York, NY: Plenum.

Schwartz, L.L. (1989, June). *Suddenly single—at mid-life and after.* Paper presented at the annual meeting of the International Council of Psychologists, Halifax, Nova Scotia.

Wiseman, R.S. (1975). Crisis theory and the process of divorce. *Social Casework, 56*(4), 205–212.

—Lita Linzer Schwartz, PhD
Editor

Biographies

Lita Linzer Schwartz (PhD, Bryn Mawr College) is Distinguished Professor of Educational Psychology at Penn State, Ogontz Campus. A diplomate in Forensic Psychology, her primary interests in this field include child custody (in adoption and divorce), family law, divorce mediation, children's rights, and questions related to overcoming infertility (e.g., surrogate motherhood).

She is author or co-author of more than a dozen books, including *The Dynamics of Divorce* (with F.W. Kaslow), *The American School and the Melting Pot* (with N. Isser), and *Alternatives to Infertility*, as well as 70 + articles on the effects of divorce on children, creativity, women in the work world, and religious cults. In addition to the monograph in hand, Schwartz is currently writing a book on education of the gifted (and hopes to do a book on photography someday).

Jon Carlson, PsyD, EdD, is Distinguished Professor at Governors State University in University Park, Illinois, and director of the Lake Geneva, Wisconsin Wellness Clinic. Dr. Carlson has served as the president of the International Assocation of Marriage and Family Counselors. He has authored 16 books and over 100 professional articles. He serves as the editor of *Individual Psychology: The Journal of Adlerian Theory, Research, and Practice*, as well as *The Family Journal*. He holds a diplomate in Family Psychology from the American Board of Professional Psychology. He is a Fellow of the American Psychological Association, a clinical member of AAMFT, and a certified sex therapist by AASECT. He has received awards for his professional contributions from the American Counseling Association, American Psychological Association, North American Society of Adlerian Psychology, and the International Association of Marriage and Family Counselors. Dr. Carlson and his wife of 25 years, Laura, are the parents of five children.

Contributors

Timothy H. Brubaker, PhD, is a Professor in the Family and Child Studies Center, Miami University, Oxford, Ohio.

Bruce Fisher, EdD, is Director at Family Relations Learning Center, Boulder, Colorado.

Charles B. Hennon, PhD, is a Professor in the Family and Child Studies Center, Miami University, Oxford, Ohio.

Florence W. Kaslow, PhD, is Director at the Florida Couples and Family Institute, West Palm Beach, Florida. She is also Visiting Professor of Medical Psychology in Psychiatry at Duke University Medical Center and Visiting Professor of Psychology at the Florida Institute of Technology.

Diana Adile Kirschner, PhD, is in private practice and on the faculty of the Wharton School, Division of Family Business Studies, University of Pennsylvania, Philadelphia.

Sam Kirschner, PhD, is in private practice and on the faculty of the Wharton School, Division of Family Business Studies, University of Pennsylvania, Philadelphia.

Carol L. Philpot, PsyD, is Associate Professor and Associate Director at the Clinical Training Program, Florida Institute of Technology, Melbourne, Florida.

Martina Reaves, JD, is an Attorney/Mediator, Emeryville, California.

Peter D. Rogers, PhD, is Psychologist/Mediator at Families in Transition, San Francisco, California.

Walter M. Schackman, BA, JD, LLM, is an Acting Supreme Court Justice for the State of New York.

Sidney David Segal, EdD, is a Lecturer in Education at Pennsylvania State University, Ogontz Campus, Abington, Pennsylvania.

PART **I**

BASIC ISSUES
OF MID-LIFE DIVORCE

1

Mid-Life Divorce: His and Hers

Carol L. Philpot, PsyD

Mid-life divorce generally conjures up visions of a silver-haired man in his early 50s running off in his red Corvette with a blonde half his age, leaving behind his dowdy, depressed wife of 20 years and angry young adult children. But this is only one of many different scenarios encountered in actual practice. There is also an equal number of abandoned men whose wives give up on them in mid-life for one reason or another and move on. In fact Zeiss, Zeiss, and Johnson (1980) reported that women are more likely to initiate divorce than are men. An examination of the files of my own practice over the past 7 years reveals 25 wife-initiated divorces compared with 22 husband-initiated ones. Interestingly, however, 14 (66.6%) of the husbands were engaged in an affair with another woman prior to the divorce, whereas only 7 (28%) of the wives had an outside relationship. Regardless of whether the men were involved with someone else, they complained that their wives were sexually unattractive or inhibited; boring, shallow, and unintelligent; or bitchy, demanding, and controlling. Women's complaints fell into three categories: (a) the inability of their spouses to relate on an intimate level; (b) the ineffectual functioning of passive-dependent or passive-aggressive spouses; or (c) the controlling, domineering nature of sexist spouses, including, in extreme cases, spouse abuse. Obviously, both the structure and etiology of mid-life divorce are varied and complex. This chapter attempts to address the differential motives for divorce as well as its impact on men and women at

mid-life. Implications both for therapeutic interventions and, idealis-
tically, sociological change are offered.

Mid-Life Developmental Tasks

Almost 35% of all divorces occurring in the 1980s involved people
between the ages of 35 and 55 (Hacker, 1983; Weitzman, 1981).
Although recent research (Ciernia, 1985) does not support the notion
that mid-life presents increased risk of divorce over younger ages,
life-cycle theories of development aid in the understanding of those
divorces that do occur at this stage.

Building on Freud's original model of children's psychosexual
stages of development, Erikson (1963) identified stages of development for adults, which designate certain tasks to be completed
during each period in order to move on successfully to the next.
The first of these is identity versus role confusion, occurring in the
late teens and early 20s, a period of time during which many marriages take place. It is fairly well established in family theory (Bowen,
1978; Dicks, 1963; Scarf, 1988) and is certainly corroborated in my
own clinical experience that only when individuals achieve a sound
identity of their own are they able to risk total intimacy with another
without fear of losing themselves. If this task is not well navigated,
the next stage, intimacy versus isolation, will suffer as well. It is
easy to predict that a marriage contracted before a solid identity
has been formed, thus resulting in a lack of intimacy, is at risk of
being discarded or at the very least redefined by the time adults
reach the mid-life task of generativity versus stagnation.

In *Seasons of a Mans Life*, Levinson (1978) described the life
stages of the adult male, the result of a longitudinal study of 40
males from all walks of life. He found that men in their middle years
(ages 45–55) are coming to grips with their limitations in life and
are evaluating the potential to recoup their losses. Having devoted
their early years to career development, they are either satisfied
with their successes and ready to devote time to neglected areas
of their lives, especially relationships with family and friends, or
are disillusioned with the rewards of the work world and turn to
family relationships for comfort. Either way, mid-life seems to be
a time when men move more toward emotional expressiveness,
nurturance, and relationships. Levinson is presently working on a
similar longitudinal study of females, the results of which have
not been published. However, preliminary reports (Levinson, 1987)
indicate that women, like men, upon evaluation at mid-life, tend to
focus their energy on developing the neglected portions of their

lives. For many, this would indicate an emphasis on career and achievement outside the home.

Others (Guttman, 1977; Lowenthal, Thurner, & Chiriboga, 1975; Mitchell & Helson, 1990; Moreland, 1980; Neugarten & Guttman, 1958; Zube, 1982) have found that a gender role convergence takes place at mid-life where men move toward relationships and women move toward autonomy and achievement. Interestingly, Mitchell and Helson found that women who rated their lives as most satisfying at mid-life essentially had achieved autonomy concurrently with an intimate relationship, indicating support for the notion that androgyny may indeed be linked to a successful negotiation of the generativity versus stagnation stage of development.

Regardless, both genders appear to assess their lives at regular intervals and attempt to correct the components that are less satisfying. What makes mid-life somewhat more disruptive is that, due to the aging process and the value our society puts on youth, individuals' options are narrowing. For many people, a sense of urgency, an "its now or never" mentality, develops, which may engender more risk-taking behavior than might occur at earlier stages. Thus, both men and women who are dissatisfied with their marital relationship are at risk for divorce. For a woman who has moved out successfully into the competitive marketplace, a newfound self-confidence and an ability to provide herself with economic security dissuades her from wasting any more time in a less than fulfilling relationship. For a man who is looking more toward relationships for fulfillment and is beginning to experience both the physical limitations of aging and the tapering off of career advancement, what better rejuvenation is there than a relationship with a new woman who sees him through adoring eyes rather than the realistic appraisal of his wife of 20 years?

Of course, human development does not occur in a vacuum. Both the familial and social context play an important role. Carter and McGoldrick (1980), in their conceptualization of the family developmental life cycle, described the mid-life period as one in which parents must launch their children, redefine their relationship, and deal with the problems of aging parents. Similar to other developmental theorists, Carter and McGoldrick suggested that when the developmental task is left incomplete in one stage, it will crop back up in the transition period of another stage. Parents who have not formed a strong bond before their children are born will need to readdress that issue when their children have moved out and are no longer at home to serve as a buffer or unification. Often, they will simply decide there is little foundation to build on, and, viewing the task as monumental, opt instead to find a new mate.

Children leaving home can free the mother, who has been the primary caregiver, to follow her own pursuits, a situation that often results in the woman's completing the developmental task of finding her own identity three decades late. Because women are socialized to sacrifice themselves for the good of the family, their own goals, values, plans, and dreams are often put on the back burner until the children are launched. For many women, mid-life is the first time they identify themselves as something other than wife and mother. The newfound identity may or may not fit well with that of their spouse of 20 or more years. It is interesting that Rice and Rice (1986) saw marriage as having an impact on both developing one's own identity and achieving intimacy. They viewed divorce as a natural developmental stage during which one continues work on both of those processes.

Also at this stage, mid-life adults are dealing with the physical deterioration of their parents, which has the effect of making them aware of their mortality and the limited time they have left to enjoy life. Dissatisfaction with a marriage, especially one that has been unfulfilling over a long period of time, leads to a "cut your losses; life is too short" philosophy, which provides justification for a divorce.

Gender Socialization

Western patriarchal society endorses values and gender role stereotypes that set the stage for major dissatisfaction of both genders with marriage at mid-life. Traditionally, women have been socialized to be homemakers and mothers and to provide for the needs of both husband and children, whereas men have been taught to compete in the world of business to provide financial support for the family. The rewards of marriage for a man are guaranteed sex, emotional support, an efficiently and smoothly run home, and children whose upbringings are essentially left up to his wife. For the woman, the major reward is economic security for herself and her children. Although she too hoped for emotional support and intimacy, the man is not socialized to be emotionally expressive. The very skills and traits that make men successful in business (i.e., aggressive, competitive, dominant, controlled, rational, rigid) make them poor nurturers and listeners. Indeed, emotional expression is thwarted in little boys, so much so that grown men often are unaware of and cannot identify feelings (other than anger) they do have. Emotion is equated with weakness. Little wonder then that women find their husbands emotionally distant and unable to sustain intimacy.

Men are socialized to place their own careers and plans in top priority, often with the genuine belief that what is best for them is also best for the family. Women are socialized to be flexible, to accommodate to others' needs, and to find their happiness in relationship to others. Society, however, rewards men with money and power and, by omission of financial reward, diminishes the role of women. Women who have chosen to devote their lives to children and family feel undervalued by society, second-class citizens whose priorities always come after those of their families. The work they do is usually repetitive and generally relegated to the lower echelons of society. They are often understimulated intellectually and isolated from the world of commerce and politics, their opinions ignored, and their needs trivialized. Little wonder, then, that their husbands find them boring and unintelligent.

The result is that women are depressed, angry, confused, and often feel guilty that they do not appreciate the role that society has given them. The relationship between marriage and depression in women has been well established (Mowbray, Lanir, & Hulce, 1984; Sobel & Russo, 1981). Indeed, the literature shows clearly that marriage increases both the mental and physical health of men and reduces both for women (Barnett, Biener, & Baruch, 1987; Bograd, 1984; Goldner, Penn, Sheinberg, & Walker, 1990; McGoldrick, Anderson, & Walsh, 1989; Mowbray et al., 1984; Sobel & Russo, 1981; Walker, 1979; Whisman & Jacobson, 1989). Women who are depressed or in ill health and who have poor self-concepts and feel worthless often do not take pride in their appearance and are uninterested in sex. Little wonder, then, that their husbands find them sexually unattractive.

Women who work outside the home, whether out of necessity, for intellectual stimulation, or psychological reasons (i.e., so as to feel more valued by society), have found themselves still shouldering the lion's share of household responsibility and child care (Hochschild, 1989). They are exhausted, angry, and resentful. Little wonder, then, that their husbands find them bitchy and demanding.

Men are also socialized to believe that they should be in control—should wear the pants in the family, so to speak. In conjunction with this, men expect to have the most prestigious jobs, make the most money, and have the greatest influence in decision making. In some subcultures of our society, if a man can't keep his wife and children under control, he is humiliated by his peers. The man who has the least psychological or intellectual sophistication, the least real power, has fewer resources to maintain this control and often resorts to physical abuse. Little wonder, then, that women find their husbands domineering and even abusive.

If a man's wife is more successful than he in the business world, he feels like a failure. It takes a very emotionally mature and secure man to accommodate to his wife's career in a world where *real* men support their families financially, not emotionally. More likely, the man will seek out someone with whom he can feel powerful and superior again, probably a younger, less secure woman. On the other hand, a man who takes a passive-dependent role with his more successful and dominant wife is not appreciated by her either. She too has been taught to expect the man to be the boss and devalues a man who willingly takes the subservient role. Little wonder, then, that women complain of passive-dependent husbands, a role that women have occupied with society's approval for centuries.

Our society values youth and beauty in women, money and power in men. In a society that overemphasizes the sexual utility of women and the earning power of men, the value of men increases with age; for women, it decreases.

All of these factors converge at mid-life. Both men and women are disillusioned with the bill of goods they were sold in their 20s. Both are struggling with unresolved issues from past developmental stages. Both are looking at ways to correct the unfulfilled aspects of their lives. Both are becoming aware of the unexpressed portions of their personalities. Both are victims of their socialization. No wonder, then, that research shows that marital satisfaction declines in the first 20 years of marriage to its lowest point during the middle years (Anderson, Russell, & Schumm, 1983; Rollins & Cannon, 1974). Given these obstacles, it seems a miracle that any marriages make it through mid-life at all.

The Six Divorces of Mid-Life

Just as the genders approach mid-life divorce from different perspectives, so do they survive the experience differently. Bohannon (1970) developed a framework for examining divorce that divides the process into six separate divorces: (a) emotional, (b) legal, (c) economic, (d) co-parental, (e) community, and (f) psychic. This conceptualization provides a good organization by which to look at the differential impact of the multifaced process of mid-life divorce on men and women.

The Emotional Divorce

According to Bohannon, the emotional divorce is the period of time during which either or both partners become increasingly aware of their disillusionment with one another and begin to see the other in negative terms. It is completed when a spouse has come to accept that there is no viable future with the other partner and becomes emotionally invested in other interests. It is intuitively obvious that in most cases initiators of divorce are those who have already begun the detachment process, and, of course, initiation of divorce has been shown to be associated with better divorce adjustment and moderate improvement in quality of life experienced long after divorce (Kurdek & Blisk, 1983; Pettit & Bloom, 1984; Wallerstein, 1986).

An interesting phenomenon reported by numerous investigators is that women, presumably because of their interest in and gender role assignment of maintaining the relationship, are more likely to experience the predivorce period as stressful (Baruch, Barnett, & Rivers, 1983; Bloom & Caldwell, 1981; Chiriboga & Cutler, 1977) and are more likely than men to be able to identify problems in the marriage predivorce (Thurnher, Fenn, Melichar, & Chiriboga, 1983). For them, the emotional divorce begins as much as several years before initiation of the legal divorce. Men are more likely to be unaware of marital problems and perceive the divorce as coming as a complete surprise (Kurdek & Blisk, 1983; Pettit & Bloom, 1984; Thomas, 1982; Zeiss et al., 1980). This concurs with the marital interaction described by Gottman (1989) in which a man begins to stonewall his wife to protect himself from the physiological arousal that occurs as a result of conflict with her. She continues to escalate the complaints until she becomes totally disgusted with him, at which point she gives up trying. For women who initiate divorce in mid-life, the emotional divorce has often occurred before the legal one begins.

L.C., a 45-year-old nurse married to her husband, J., for 25 years, came to therapy complaining that she had no feeling left for him. She stated that he did not know how to be intimate or to communicate about anything that was important to her. She preferred the company of her women friends who knew her better and gave her more emotional support than she could ever expect from J. She wondered whether all long-term marriages were like this, or whether she was justified in leaving J. even though he made a good living, wasn't particularly contentious, and was considered a good man by her friends. She described her relationship with him as dead and felt she would be happier alone. L.C. was emotionally divorced, whereas her husband J. didn't even know a problem existed. He was totally baffled by her threat to leave and stated that although he remembered some vague complaints in the past, he never took them seriously. This is a typical scenario in my practice.

For men like J., the emotional divorce extends from the time of the wife's pronouncement to as long as 3 to 5 years after the breakup (Weiss, 1975). Men in general, whether they are initiators of divorce, report feeling a greater degree of attachment and a desire to reconcile (Bloom & Kindle, 1985; Brown & Reimer, 1984; Zeiss et al., 1980). Attachment, defined as an emotional dependence on the ex-spouse, is negatively related to adjustment (Kitson, 1982). These men go through the usual stages of grief—denial, anger, bargaining, depression, and acceptance—but they are not fully emotionally divorced until they reach the final stage. Their struggle through the grief process can take several forms, ranging from violent anger through passive-aggressive manipulations to dependency and severe depression.

Formation of a new relationship is the most common way to deal with emotional divorce (Furstenberg & Spanier, 1984; Spanier & Thompson, 1984), and for many men this occurs before the legal divorce is initiated. For the majority of these men, the emotional divorce has been going on for many years within the marriage and the other woman is merely the catalyst that provides him with the support to finally leave.

> B. came to therapy essentially to ask me to take care of his wife, W., of 30 years when he finally broke the news to her that he wanted a divorce. B. had found another woman who seemed to appreciate him and respect him, one who did not criticize him constantly, and one who supported herself. He had come to see W. as critical, whining, demanding, and dependent—basically a stone around his neck. However, he was grateful to this "excellent housewife and mother" for raising their four children who were now grown and independent, and he recognized her helplessness to take care of herself. He was struggling with strong feelings of guilt, obligation, and fear of alienating his friends, parents, and children. On the other hand, he experienced an urgency to "grab the golden ring" before it was too late. He believed this new relationship offered him a new lease on life. He was tormented and conflicted, which manifested itself in emotional liability and inability to concentrate at work. His wife, W., was both frightened and outraged at this development, and put most of her energy for the next several years into hating him and creating an army of supporters for her plight. She felt she had sacrificed her whole life for him, and now that she was "used up" and "unwanted," he was abandoning her for a younger woman.

This is the other common scenario in my practice. In this case, it is the wife whose emotional divorce is prolonged, taking the form of extreme anger, rather than longing and depression. However, women work toward detachment interaction with ex-spouses (Goetting, 1979; Spanier & Thompson, 1984) even when they are not the initiators. They are also more likely to find emotional support with family and friends, which helps to alleviate some distress and feelings of isolation (Chiriboga, Coho, Stein, & Roberts, 1979; Keith, 1986). Davis and Aron (1988) found that women in mid-life who attribute the end of their marriages to failings of their spouses rather than blame themselves show a better postdivorce adjustment, because such an attribution serves to protect their wounded self-esteems. For women in mid-life, however, the option of forming a new romantic attachment is less viable due to society's devaluation of women over 40 as sexual objects, a factor that contributes to prolonged emotional divorce. The inequity for men and women at this stage in life creates in women a sense of helpless fury that is very powerful. Women who can find a substitute on which to focus their emotional energy, whether it be children, friends, support group, volunteer work, or career, emerge from the emotional divorce stage more quickly. Indeed, Warfield (cited in Colborn, 1991) found that after divorce, professional women do cope with their new status and emotions by throwing themselves into their careers, whereas men tend to have poorer job performance and more absences. It's as if once the decision to divorce is made, much of women's emotional energy is freed up to be focused on work, whereas men do not focus energy on the relationship until divorce is imminent.

However, for both men and women who divorce at mid-life, the initiator has the advantage of preparation time and some control over the situation, whereas his or her spouse complains of the unilateral decision that has disrupted his or her whole life. Unexpected negative events produce feelings of loss of control and concomitant anxiety (Langer, 1983; Lazarus & Folkman, 1984; Wortman, 1983), which naturally impair positive adjustment to divorce.

The Legal Divorce

Kressel (1985) argued that women may be at a disadvantage when it comes to the legal divorce. It is fairly easy to understand why. Most women do not concern themselves enough with the financial affairs of their husband's business nor even with their own family finances. They understand little about tax laws, investments, pension plans, and so forth. Neither do they know what the present divorce laws entitle them to and what they are likely to lose. When the divorce occurs, it is important for the woman, who feels inadequate, to obtain professional advice. However, accountants and lawyers who have served the family in the past can only represent the husband or wife, and because the husband is generally the person with the money, they will remain loyal to him. This then requires the woman to look elsewhere for counsel and to depend on the recommendations of friends who have been through this before, a process that does not have guaranteed results. Furthermore, the husband can generally afford pricey lawyers whose reputations precede them. Unless the husband is very well to do and the lawyer thinks his client has a chance of getting a large settlement from which she will be able to pay him, the expensive, competent lawyer will not wish to represent the wife.

At the bargaining table, a lack of knowledge, economic dependence, and fear of conflict can hamper a woman's ability to negotiate in her best interests. For the woman who has no source of income other than her husband's good will during separation, his refusal to help her financially until the judge makes a determination in the case can coerce her into making agreements that are unfavorable to her. Kressel indicated that in a competitive encounter with the opposite gender, women are less powerful than men.

Divorce laws were not made with the middle-aged woman in mind. Presently, most settlements either do not include alimony, or provide "rehabilitative alimony" intended to prepare the woman to enter the workplace. For the woman in mid-life, this is an unrealistic expectation. These women must be aware of their ability to ask for continued health benefits, portions of pension plans, career assets, and lost career opportunities. They must be concerned about their ability to establish credit ratings. They must realize that tax laws can greatly affect benefits as well. In one case, a woman who had received what appeared to be a fairly equitable settlement found that when the family home was sold 3 years after she had moved out, she had to pay capital gains tax on her 50% of the profit because for her this had become investment property, whereas her ex-husband, age 55, was able to reinvest in a new home within 2 years without paying tax.

In cases where young children are involved, I generally recommend divorce mediation so that the couple can have more control over their own settlement and will hopefully develop the spirit of cooperation needed to co-parent their children. However, in the case of the middle-aged woman who is unsophisticated in the world of finance, I highly recommend she consult both a good lawyer and a competent accountant. Of course, the real solution to this problem is for the woman to make herself knowledgeable about such matters and stop expecting the man to handle the family finances.

On the other hand, in custody disputes, the man is generally at a disadvantage. However, at mid-life, children are usually independent, or older adolescents who essentially choose with whom they would prefer to live. Therefore, mid-life fathers do not feel the same sense of hopelessness over legal decisions that impair their ability to interact with and have an impact on their children experienced by men with dependent, younger children. (This does not mean that mid-life fathers have smooth sailing with their children. See the section on co-parenting.)

The Economic Divorce

If middle-aged women fare better than their male counterparts in the emotional divorce, they are definitely the losers in the economic divorce. Weitzman (1985) eloquently pointed out the economic inequity in the new no-fault divorce laws when applied to middle-aged women who have been married 15 years or more. This is most drastic for those women who have been full-time housewives with no job training, whose children are over 18, and whose husbands make less than $20,000 a year when no alimony or child support is awarded. Welfare may be her only support. However, even in cases where some child support or alimony is awarded, the middle-aged woman's financial resources are drastically reduced from predivorce standards.

The reasons for this are multiple. First, women typically make 60% less money than men in our society, even when they are trained (Morgan, 1991; Weitzman, 1985). Second, women who have devoted most of their lives to raising children have typically not developed a career track, but have worked part-time jobs that have accommodated their children's and husband's schedules, which relegates them to lower income positions. Men in mid-life are generally at the prime of their careers, and their income potential is many times greater than their wives'. If adolescent children are still in the home, they generally live with their mothers, who support them. Per capita median income when all members of the household are considered is about 24% of the predivorce income for wives and 87% for husbands (Weitzman, 1985). Husbands are notorious for reneging on alimony and child support payments, which are difficult to enforce. An already poverty-stricken woman does not have the funds to retain legal help to fight for back payments. Alimony payments today are often awarded on a declining schedule, supposedly to give the woman time to get back into the workforce. However, even if she uses the rehabilitative alimony to better her education for a job, she still faces an unwelcome job market that has no interest in hiring a middle-aged woman who has no experience. When one takes into account all of the benefits that generally accompany the husband's employment (e.g., medical insurance, expense accounts, country club membership, pension plans, etc.) and that the wife gives up in divorce, the economic toll is even greater. Income for women will rise with remarriage. However, the chance for remarriage in women is only 28% after the age of 40.

The woman who is now divorcing at mid-life believed she was entering a contract by which she would provide for the emotional and nurturing needs of her husband and children while he would provide the income to support them. To find at mid-life that her investment in his career was a total waste is the ultimate injustice. Even when a man makes enough money to provide his ex-spouse with a livable alimony and makes the payments (14%–15% of all divorces), by 1 year after divorce, her standard of living is typically reduced by an average of 73% of what it had been during marriage, whereas his, although initially reduced by one third, actually increases by 42%.

> M.J., at 58, is working for $5.72 an hour as a clerk/typist in a local school. She received rehabilitative alimony for 3 years after her divorce, during which she took courses in a vocational school to prepare herself as a secretary. She owns her own home, which she won in the divorce settlement 10 years ago, but has no money for repairs, so the house is in appalling condition. She has no health benefits and minimal car insurance. She drives a 10-year-old car that needs constant repair. She has no credit cards, buys her clothes at Goodwill, and never eats out. She dreads becoming ill because she cannot afford a physician. She cannot afford make-up, hairdressers, or nice clothes, and so appears less attractive than she really is. She has two grown children who rarely visit her because she depresses them. She is emotionally labile and severely depressed, and her chances of finding a new husband in her present condition are very slim. Her ex-husband lives in a split-level, well-kept home with his second wife. He drives a late-model Oldsmobile, and his wife has a compact car. They take frequent vacations and maintain an active social life. Both husband and second wife can afford moderately expensive clothes, a health club, and the beauty parlor, and hence look younger and more attractive than M.J. does. M.J. was a housewife and mother of two who made the mistake of having an affair at age 45 and got caught!

Only women who have worked continuously at a career during their marriage fare well economically. Morgan (1991) found that education and stable work history were the best predictors of avoidance of poverty for middle-aged, divorced women. The implications for young women marrying today are clear. Put your career in top priority, and do not accommodate to your husband's or your children's needs because the consequences of playing wife and mother can be severe.

This is not to say that men do not suffer economically as well. It simply is not possible to provide for two households as cheaply as one, and the legal process of divorce can be very expensive. Frequently, men are angered at being asked to provide for a lifetime for women whom they no longer love, especially when they begin to incur new expenses with a second family. Indeed, some men will lose interest in working with advancement and higher salary if they feel such raises will have to be shared with ex-spouses and instead merely drift at work or quit altogether. Nevertheless, in a patriarchal society, the potential income for males is always higher than that for females, and they at least have the security of a regular paycheck, if they wish to work.

The Co-Parental Divorce

Although parents at mid-life do not generally get involved with heated custody battles, even adolescent and adult children can become triangulated between angry parents. Adolescents who are still living at home will be more influenced by the primary residential parent and his or her attitude both toward the ex-spouse and toward that particular gender in general. This is particularly damaging when a mother portrays all men as bastards to her son, or when a father expresses hatred of all women to his daughter. The natural implication is that the child is also unlovable. When there is extreme anger, any interaction of children with the ex-spouse is perceived as betrayal. Often, then, adolescent children are forced to take sides, or at the very least keep secret any feelings of love or longing for the missing parent. If the residential parent is emotionally labile, as is often the case during the stress of divorce, adolescent and parent may reverse roles, with the adolescent taking on the responsibility of supporting and advising the adult. If the residential parent is actively dating, the overt sexuality of his or her parent is often disturbing to the adolescent who is also in the process of experimenting with sexuality. Adolescents may take advantage of the reduced emotional and psychological resources of a stressed parent to act out in typical teenaged rebellion, such as cutting school, drinking, becoming sexually active, taking drugs, or even shoplifting or vandalizing property. If this happens, often the noncustodial parent will ask for or be given custody of the rebellious child in hopes of curbing the behavior.

Parents may need to cooperate in setting limits and problem-solving regarding the problems of their adolescents, but this may be particularly hard to accomplish when emotions of anger, betrayal, and distrust run high. In general, adolescents seem to prefer to live with the same-gender parent who can provide them with a role model. If this is not possible, a same-gender adult relative, teacher, friend, or coach becomes an important person in the adolescent's life. Many times, adolescents begin by living with the mother, whose emotional, psychological, and economic resources are severely strained already, and move to the father only when the mother can no longer cope. An added problem for children who live with their mother is that they share the same reduction of income often to the point of poverty that their mother experiences (see previous section). This creates great resentment for the father, who seems to them to be living on easy street. His lack of concern for their reduced economic circumstances is viewed as abandonment.

The initiator of the divorce (with the exception of a woman escaping from an abusive relationship) will often bear the brunt of his or her children's anger. This is understandable. Children, unless they have been subjected to intense arguments and violence, would prefer that the marriage remain intact. The perpetrator of divorce has made a decision over which the children have had no control, but that drastically disrupts their lives. This appears to them to be totally selfish, and parents are not supposed to be selfish.

Even when children are adults and independent, problems arise when parents harbor a great deal of anger. Again, adult children are afraid to talk about the ex-spouse in front of the other parent for fear that any show of affection for one spouse might betray the other. When either or both parents confide their pain and hurt in their adult children, openly criticizing the ex-spouse, adult children are put in the awkward position of either defending the absent parent or colluding with the present one. On special occasions, such as weddings and graduations, tension between the ex-partners can cause the children to invite only one parent to avoid open conflict and thus painfully neglect the other. Any influence of the other parent in the adult child's life can be resented. New partners are often a source of real discomfort for adult children who know intellectually that parents must go on with their lives, but emotionally still think they should be together. Acceptance of a new spouse is even more a betrayal of the ex-spouse if there was an affair before the marriage ended. In general, when both spouses have remarried and emotionally detached from the other, the tensions are reduced, and relationships are easier.

Wright and Maxwell (1991) found that divorced mothers receive significantly more support than fathers from their adult children in four areas: (a) advice, (b) services, (c) financial assistance, and (d) socioemotional aid. These results seemed to be related to the greater frequency of interaction with mothers, greater emotional closeness with mothers, and mothers' expectation of support and greater financial strain. Fathers do not appear to turn to their children for emotional or financial help, and children do not generally perceive their fathers as in need of support.

Although many fathers lose contact with their adult children, others develop adult relationships with them that exceed the closeness they had predivorce. Fathers have traditionally communicated with their children in an instructional or critical manner while allowing their mothers to provide them with nurturance. A divorce can often bring a man in touch with his feelings; therapy can teach him to communicate more expressively. Because he can no longer use his children's mother as a go-between, he may learn how to communicate with them directly on an intimate level for the first time.

The Community Divorce

Divorce invariably disrupts old roles in the social community to which a couple once belonged. Many of the activities people engage in as a couple are no longer available to them as divorcees. Old friends are torn between the couple, sometimes taking sides, and sometimes avoiding both partners in order to appear neutral. Inviting both spouses to the same event can be awkward, so choices have to be made. The initiator is likely to be considered the villain who needs or deserves no help, whereas the victim is often the recipient of the support. On the other hand, listening to the litany of offenses committed by the ex-spouse can become tedious for old friends who may back off from the newly separated altogether. Other divorcees isolate themselves because they do not wish to subject their friends to their state of depression or talk about their divorce. For the newly divorced woman who was once her husband's hostess and companion for a variety of organizational social events, the loss of his professional network can leave a big gap. For the man whose ex-wife organized his social life and provided the reciprocity for social engagements, entertaining others becomes a dilemma, particularly if he is financially strapped postdivorce. Another interesting phenomenon that may result in isolation for the divorced partners is the contagion of divorce. That is, when one couple in a tight-knit group divorces, it often stimulates similar urges in other couples who are less than satisfied with their marriages. Contact with the divorcee, then, particularly if he or she appears to be happy, threatens the stability of his or her friends' marriages. All of this is particularly difficult for the couple who has lived for 20 years in the same community and must continue to do so after divorce.

Divorced men often find themselves in demand, particularly at mid-life. Statistics indicate that by the time of mid-life, there are more single women than men, and usually friends know several single women who would like to meet a newly divorced man. Married women often pity the bachelor who has no one to cook, clean, or do laundry for him and try to mother him. Also, because women tend to be the social organizers, they are often more comfortable inviting the male half of the couple than the female half, which they may perceive as a threat to their own marriage, especially if the woman is attractive and flirtatious.

One of the reasons women seem to handle the emotional aspects of divorce better than do men is that women generally have a social network of friends that they use for support. Men have been socialized to hide their vulnerability and do not seek out emotional support as readily as do women. Furthermore, most men have only superficial relationships with their male friends with whom they are uncomfortable sharing their pain, which they equate with weakness. Frequently, the depressed divorced male will become isolated and engage in destructive behaviors such as alcohol abuse during the adjustment period. Because for many men, the only person in whom they have confided has been their now estranged wife, male divorcees will often attach themselves quickly to a substitute "wife," a new woman confidante. They must be careful that they do not precipitously enter a new marriage based on dependency and need.

For both males and females, the more involved in activities and the more interests they have, the more likely they are to not experience overwhelming loneliness. The woman in mid-life who has devoted her time to the household and has no outside activities is particularly hampered in her ability to develop new friendships. Support groups for the widowed and divorced can often be helpful here. The workplace, volunteer work, serving on boards of directors for community institutions, health clubs, civic organizations, community theater, and so on provide a place to meet others in a less threatening atmosphere than the "meat market" in the bar scene.

Although men and women in mid-life are not hampered with small children who prevent them from getting out, they may feel their aloneness even more acutely because they do not have the distraction of child care. Both men and women at mid-life may be uncomfortable with the dating scene and particularly with sexual experimentation after 20 years with the same partner. This is even more dangerous in the days of acquired immunodeficiency syndrome (AIDS) and herpes.

The world of friendships and organizations is not the only one that is disrupted by divorce, however. Even more problematic is the relationship with former in-laws, particularly in the case of a long-term marriage during which intimacy and dependency has had time to develop. Indeed, there will be times when the parents are opposed to the divorce initiated by their own adult child and will actually side with the daughter- or son-in-law. This is quite painful to the natural child who feels betrayed by his or her own parents. In some cases, it is this very concern that has kept the initiator in an unfulfilling relationship for such a long time. I am reminded of the cartoon that shows two people in their 80s who are finally divorcing after many miserable years. They explain that they have been waiting not only for their parents to die, but for their children to die, before feeling free to separate. Obviously, the predivorce relationship with one's ex-in-laws is a contributing factor to postdivorce interaction, but even in the case where predivorce relationships were close, it is sometimes difficult for parents to remain neutral.

> K., a 43-year-old woman, separated from her husband of 20 years and embroiled in divorce litigation, was hurt that her estranged mother-in-law deliberately ignored her birthday. This was particularly painful for her because her mother-in-law had been her confidante and support for over a decade, and she felt more affection and caring for her than for her own mother. She had always felt that love was reciprocated. As it turned out, her mother-in-law had heard only her son's side of the marital dispute and saw K. as the initiator and villain. She was unable to get past the anger to try to understand K.'s position.

Although it is less imperative to children's welfare once they are grown and independent to maintain a cooperative relationship with the ex-in-laws, there will still be occasions, such as weddings and graduations, when ex-spouses will need to interact with the extended family. This will be more comfortable for all if hatchets can be buried and neutrality maintained.

The Psychic Divorce

The psychic divorce refers to the identity problems that occur due to a divorce. For the mid-life woman who has identified herself as the doctor's wife or the professor's wife for 20 years, this can be a traumatic experience. She is no longer treated with the respect that was once accorded her due to her marital connection. Furthermore, reduced income often plummets her into poverty, and the woman who used to shop at Saks is buying her clothes at WalMart. She no longer belongs to the clubs she once did, she can no longer eat out with friends, and she no longer has the money for hobbies. If she has adolescent children, her identification as mother may still be intact, but it is changing in nature, and soon her services will be less needed. Unless she has a career identification or enough money to maintain past recreational and civic connections, she is no longer who she was. She is in danger of living only in the past if she cannot find a new purpose for living. Helping the mid-life woman create a new identity with a clear raison d'etre is a major task of therapists. Although men tend to identify themselves more with their occupations than with their relationships, they too can have problems of identity that emerge out of a broken marriage.

> M., a 52-year-old physician, had worked all his life toward an early retirement. His dream for the future included retiring to the mountains and entertaining his grandchildren while he sat in his rocker on the front porch. At mid-life, his wife of 25 years left him because he was emotionally and physically unavailable. His sense of direction was jarred. He was suddenly thrust into a dating world as a single man. He had no desire to start over again with someone new. He wanted his old dream back. He did not think of himself as a much in demand eligible bachelor, but a laid-back and relaxed grandfather.

Although therapists generally help the divorced to understand how they contributed to their marital problems so that the disrupted relationship can become a learning experience to prevent problems in future partnerships, Weingarten (1988) found that individuals in mid-life must be able to develop an understanding of their divorce that preserves an image of themselves as being "okay." This is probably because they have less time to correct and improve their lives and little incentive to develop a new personal identity. The thought that they may have wasted 20 years of their lives doing something wrong seems to block the achieving of integrity and lead them to despair (Erikson, 1963). This is important information for the therapist bent on helping the mid-life person face his or her own deficiencies. Unless the individual is entering a new relationship that is likely to be adversely affected by old patterns, pushing an individual at mid-life to take responsibility for the failure of his or her relationship may actually be detrimental to the client's mental health (George & Siegler, 1982; Langer, 1983; Wortman, 1976).

Therapeutic Implications

Sprenkle (1981) and Sutton (1983) delineated 10 goals for the therapist to aid the client in reaching an adaptive divorce adjustment.

These correspond roughly to the previous six divorce categories with a few additions. The first of these is acceptance of the end of the marriage, which equates with the establishment of a new identity that is not tied to the marital status or one's ex-spouse (i.e., the psychic divorce). Although it is imperative that the client define him or herself in terms of his or her present single status, it is probably unrealistic in the case of a long-term marriage to expect all attachment to the former spouse to dissolve. Ahrons (1980) pointed out the difference between pathological attachment that prevents one from moving on in life and the natural caring and friendship that can exist between people who lived together for two decades or more. The important point is that the client not hold on to hope for reconciliation nor invest in a relationship that is no more.

The second criterion is the development of a functional postdivorce relationship. This requires that the client define new boundaries between him or her and the former spouse and develop a balanced view of the ex-partner in terms of negative and positive characteristics. Past conflicts need to be resolved or put aside.

A third criterion that needs to be addressed is the emotional adjustment (i.e., the emotional divorce). Themes to be worked through in this area include issues of self-esteem, guilt, anger, control, intimacy, dependency, loneliness, and grief. Although either prolonged anger or grief can be crippling, both play an important role in recovery from divorce. Anger can be a catalyst to get the person out of depression, whereas grieving is a necessary process for letting go and building a new life.

A fourth criterion is cognitive adjustment. In most cases, the therapist attempts to help the client understand his or her contribution to the failure of the marriage and the process of mate selection so as not to repeat the same mistake again. As stated before, the attainment of this goal must be weighed against the possible loss of integrity for the older adult who must somehow preserve a sense of being "okay." To this end, it may be helpful for the client to see the termination of his or her marriage developmentally, and therefore as a natural process in growth (Rice & Rice, 1986), and as a part of a larger system, both multigenerationally and sociologically (Kaslow & Schwartz, 1987).

The fifth criterion is the development of a social support system (i.e., the community divorce). Involvement with friends, support groups, colleagues, and organizations, as well as the resumption of dating, are correlated with less stress and better adjustment. It is important, however, that the mid-life man or woman who has been accustomed to living with someone else for several decades not retreat into remarriage due to fear of loneliness.

The sixth and seventh criteria are healthy parental and children's adjustment (the co-parental divorce). Parents who can focus on the parental role, that is, not play out old conflicts through their children but keep their children's best interest in the forefront, are most likely to reach this goal. They must not compete for the children's affection, attempt to triangulate the children into their disagreements, communicate through the children, nor prevent their children from developing good relationships with new stepparents.

The eighth criterion is the use of the divorce as an opportunity for personal growth. In this area, it is clear that mid-life women generally fare very well. In spite of their severe economic difficulties, a long-lasting rise in the self-esteem of women results from divorce (Baruch et al., 1983; Haggman & Ashkenas, 1974; Wallerstein & Kelly, 1980). This is probably because these women take charge of their lives for the first time and learn how to take care of themselves physically, economically, psychologically, socially—in every way. They get in touch with their capabilities and strengths and develop an independent sense of self, which was not possible while they played the caregiving role for others. As Diedrick (1991) put it, "Perhaps it is simply that women have much to gain whereas men have little to gain after divorce in terms of self-esteem that accounts for some of the gender difference noted in postseparation adjustment" (p. 39).

But it is not just women who must learn new skills and competencies after divorce. Immediately postdivorce, many men live a chaotic life-style because they cannot cook, clean house, do laundry, shop, or accomplish any of the life-sustaining chores that their wives had previously handled for them (Hetherington, Cox, & Cox, 1978). They eat poorly, sleep erratically, and as a result suffer physical illness and poor work performance. All of these tasks must be learned. But perhaps the most important growth factor for most men is the use of therapy after divorce to learn how to allow themselves to be vulnerable and to express themselves emotionally (Scher, 1981).

The ninth criterion for adjustment is obtaining a legal settlement that is equitable and satisfactory (i.e., the legal divorce). This requires the client to be assertive in taking care of him or herself while not treating the ex-spouse unfairly. The therapist can help the client to separate feelings of guilt and/or resentment from the legal process and encourage him or her to participate as much as possible in creating the agreement. As previously stated, knowledge of financial, tax, and legal affairs gives ones client a sense of confidence to bargain more rationally and powerfully.

The final criterion is an overall measure of general life adjustment. It has been found that women report greater satisfaction and adjustment after divorce than do men despite severe financial difficulties (Albrecht, 1980; Chiriboga, 1982; Keith, 1985; Wallerstein & Kelly, 1980; Zeiss et al., 1980). Divorced males have more suicidal thoughts (Zeiss et al., 1980), higher admission rates to psychiatric hospitals (Bloom, White, & Asher, 1979), and higher mortality rates (Bloom et al., 1979) than do women. Obviously, clinicians must not underrate the pain of the divorced male simply because he has a difficult time expressing his vulnerability. Male support groups, Alcoholics Anonymous, and the new men's consciousness-raising groups may offer the male client support in this difficult adjustment.

Sociological Implications

A review of the literature regarding gender differences in divorce adjustment blatantly reveals an appalling fact: Marriage is psychologically and physically destructive to women, whereas divorce is psychologically and physically destructive to men. It's not surprising, given the structure traditional marriage has taken throughout the centuries. Until recently, marriage was an economic and political institution, and women were merely chattel. Even in the 20th century, with its romanticized view of marriage as an emotional and sexual union, there is ample documented evidence of the detrimental effect of marriage on women (Bernard, 1972; French, 1985; Friedan, 1963).

Today the Western capitalistic society is faced with the crisis of restructuring the family. Fifty percent of all marriages end in divorce. Seventy-five percent of women with small children work. The traditional family of the 1950s, composed of a working father and a housewife mother, comprise only 7% of today's families. Divorce laws make divorce easier, but no longer protect a woman who chooses to sacrifice her career for her husband and children.

A clear message is broadcast to young women who witness the typical mid-life divorce of their parents. Do as the men do. Focus your energy on a career that will fulfill you and support you economically. Keep abreast of the political, legal, and business worlds. Develop a network of friends and acquaintances who have expertise in areas you don't, and be sure you make enough money to pay them. Once you have your future secured, then and only then turn your time and energy toward your spouse and children, being careful to protect your own interests even as you accommodate to the family needs. However, if young women follow this advice, and men continue to do what they have always done, what becomes of the children? The absurd extreme result of this action would be the annihilation of the human race because no one would take time away from career to have or raise children. Yet, polls of the general population done by the popular press usually show family and children near the top of the priority list for both genders, falling right after health. It's not that people don't want the family. It's just that it desperately needs restructuring.

Young men who watch their fathers struggling with the loss of a family after 20 years of working to support it—what do they learn? Hopefully, they recognize that work isn't everything, that a relationship needs nurturing as well, that it's better not to put all your emotional eggs in one basket in case it leaves, that not expressing emotions or allowing for intimacy results in isolation, and that you don't have to wait until you lose something before you can appreciate it. Or that the S.O.B. father who left the family may not really be as cold and selfish as he seems, if he could just open up and tell people about his own pain and vulnerability. But I don't know what young men think.

● ● ●

Mid-life divorce is becoming fairly common. It is a phenomenon that therapists deal with in their offices regularly. This chapter has attempted to cover some of the issues that will evolve in divorce therapy with the mid-life couple. But mid-life divorce, like all divorce, is a symptom, like a fever. You can treat a fever with aspirin without ever knowing why the fever is there. But unless you find and correct the underlying disease, the fever will only come back.

References

Ahrons, C.R. (1980). *The continuing coparental relationship between divorced spouses.* Paper presented at the annual meeting of the American Orthopsychiatric Association, Toronto, Canada.

Albrecht, S.L. (1980). Reactions and adjustment to divorce: Differences in the experiences of males and females. *Family Relations, 29,* 59–68.

Anderson, S.A., Russell, C.S., & Schumm, W.R. (1983). Perceived marital quality and family life-cycle categories: A further analysis. *Journal of Marriage and the Family, 45,* 127–139.

Barnett, R., Biener, L., & Baruch, G. (Eds.). (1987). *Gender and stress.* New York, NY: Free Press.

Baruch, G., Barnett, R., & Rivers, C. (1983). *Lifeprints: New patterns of love and work for todays women.* New York, NY: McGraw-Hill.

Bernard, J. (1972). *The future of marriage.* New York, NY: Bantam.

Bloom, B.L., & Caldwell, R.A. (1981). Sex differences in adjustment during the process of marital separation. *Journal of Marriage & the Family, 43,* 693–701.

Bloom, B.L., & Kindle, K.R. (1985). Demographic factors in the continuing relationship between former spouses. *Family Relations, 34,* 375–381.

Bloom, B.L., White, S.W., & Asher, S.J. (1979). Marital disruption as a stressful life event. In G. Levinger & O. Moles (Eds.), *Divorce and separation: Context, causes, and consequences* (pp. 184–200). New York, NY: Basic Books.

Bograd, M. (1984). Family systems approaches to wife battering: A feminist critique. *American Journal of Orthopsychiatry, 54*(4), 558–568.

Bohannon, P. (1970). The six stations of divorce. In P. Bohannon (Ed.), *Divorce and after* (pp. 29–55). New York, NY: Anchor Books.

Bowen, M. (1978). *Family therapy in clinical practice.* New York, NY: Jason Aaronson, Inc.

Brown, S.D., & Reimer, D.A. (1984). Assessing attachment following divorce: Development and psychometric evaluation of the Divorce Reaction Inventory. *Journal of Counseling Psychology, 31,* 520–531.

Carter, E., & McGoldrick, M. (Eds.). (1980). *The family life cycle.* New York, NY: Gardner Press.

Chiriboga, D.A., (1982). Adaptation to marital separation in later and earlier life. *Journal of Gerontology, 37,* 103–114.

Chiriboga, D.A., & Cutler, L. (1977). Stress responses among divorcing men and women. *Journal of Divorce, 1,* 95–106.

Chiriboga, D.A., Coho, A., Stein, J.A., & Roberts, J. (1979). Divorce, stress and social supports: A study in helpseeking behavior. *Journal of Divorce, 3,* 121–135.

Ciernia, J.R. (1985). Myths about male midlife crises. *Psychological Reports, 56,* 1003–1007.

Colborn, M. (1991, May 17). Sexes deal differently with divorce. *Florida Today,* p. 1D.

Davis, B., & Aron, A. (1988). Perceived causes of divorce and postdivorce adjustment among recently divorced midlife women. *Journal of Divorce, 12*(1), 41–55.

Dicks, H. (1963). Object relations theory and marital studies. *British Journal of Medical Psychology, 36,* 125–129.

Diedrick, P. (1991). Gender differences in divorce adjustment. *Journal of Divorce & Remarriage, 14*(3/4), 33–45.

Erikson, E. (1963). *Childhood and society* (2nd ed.). New York, NY: Norton.

French, M. (1985). *Beyond power.* New York, NY: Ballantine.

Friedan, B. (1963). *The feminine mystique.* New York, NY: Norton.

Furstenberg, F.F., & Spanier, G.B. (1984). *Recycling the family: Remarriage after divorce.* Beverly Hills, CA: Sage.

George, L.K., & Siegler, I.C. (1982). Stress and coping in later life. *Educational Horizons,* 147–154.

Goetting, A. (1979). The normative integration of the former spouse relationship. *Journal of Divorce, 2,* 395–414.

Goldner, V., Penn, P., Sheinberg, M., & Walker, G. (1990). Love and violence: Gender paradoxes in volatile attachments. *Family Process, 29*(4), 343–364.

Gottman, J. (1989, October). *Growing up married: Men & commitment.* Plenary address at annual conference of the American Association of Marriage and Family Therapists, San Francisco, CA.

Guttman, D. (1977). The cross-sectional perspective: Notes toward a comparative psychology of aging. In J.F. Birren & K. Warren Schaie (Eds.), *Handbook of the psychology of aging.* New York, NY: Van Nostrand Reinhold.

Hacker, A. (1983). *US: A statistical portrait of the American people.* New York, NY: Viking.

Haggman, K., & Ashkenas, R. (1974, March). *Single parent study: A preliminary investigation.* Paper presented at the Massachusetts Children's Lobby Conference, Cambridge, MA.

Hetherington, E.M., Cox, M., & Cox, R. (1978). Divorced fathers. *The Family Coordinator, 25*, 417–428.

Hochschild, A. (1989). *The second shift: Working parents and the revolution at home.* New York, NY: Viking Penguin, Inc.

Kaslow, F., & Schwartz, L. (1987). *The dynamics of divorce: A lifecycle perspective.* New York, NY: Brunner/Mazel.

Keith, P.M. (1985). Financial well-being of older divorced/separated men and women: Findings from a panel study. *Journal of Divorce, 9*, 61–72.

Keith, P.M. (1986). Isolation of the unmarried in later life. *Family Relations, 35*, 389–395.

Kitson, G.C. (1982). Attachment to spouse in divorce: A scale and its application. *Journal of Marriage & the Family, 44*, 379–393.

Kressel, K. (1985). *The process of divorce.* New York, NY: Basic Books.

Kurdek, L., & Blisk, D. (1983). Dimensions and correlates of mothers' divorce experiences. *Journal of Divorce, 6*, 1–24.

Langer, E. (1983). *The psychology of control.* Beverly Hills, CA: Sage.

Lazarus, R.S., & Folkman, S. (1984). *Stress, appraisal and coping.* New York, NY: Academic Press.

Levinson, D. (1978). *Seasons of a mans life.* New York, NY: Knopf.

Levinson, D. (1987). *Seasons of a womans life.* Workshop presented at the Cape Cod Institute, Cape Cod, MA.

Lowenthal, M.F., Thurner, M., & Chiriboga, D. (1975). *Four stages of life.* San Francisco, CA: Jossey-Bass.

McGoldrick, M., Anderson, C., & Walsh, F. (Eds.). (1989). *Women in families: A framework for family therapy.* New York, NY: Norton.

Mitchell, V., & Helson, R. (1990). Women's prime of life: Is it the 50s? *Psychology of Women Quarterly, 14*, 451–470.

Moreland, J. (1980). Age and change in the adult male sex role. *Sex Roles, 6*, 807–818.

Morgan, L. (1991). *After marriage ends: Economic consequences for mid-life women.* Newbury Park, CA: Sage.

Mowbray, C., Lanir, S., & Hulce, M. (Eds.). (1984). *Women and mental health: New directions for change.* New York, NY: The Haworth Press.

Neugarten, B., & Guttman, D. (1958). Age-sex roles and personality in middle age: A thematic apperception study. *Psychology Monographs, 72.*

Pettit, E.J., & Bloom, B.L. (1984). Whose decision was it? The effects of initiator status on adjustment to marital disruption. *Journal of Marriage and the Family, 4,* 587–595.

Rice, J.K., & Rice, D.G. (1986). *Living through divorce: A developmental approach to divorce therapy.* New York, NY: Guilford.

Rollins, R.C., & Cannon, K.L. (1974). Family life cycle: A reevaluation. *Journal of Marriage and the Family, 36,* 271–282.

Scarf, M. (1988). *Intimate partners: Patterns in love and marriage.* New York, NY: Random House.

Scher, M. (1981). Men in hiding: A challenge for the counsellor. *The Personnel and Guidance Journal,* 199–202.

Sobel, S.B., & Russo, N.F. (1981). Sex roles, equality and mental health. *Professional Psychology, 12,* 1–5.

Spanier, G.B., & Thompson, L. (1984). *Parting: The aftermath of separation and divorce.* Beverly Hills, CA: Sage.

Sprenkle, D. (1981). *Is there life after divorce?* Paper presented at the Department of Child Development and Family Studies Symposium on Divorce, Purdue University, West Lafayette, IN.

Sutton, M. (1983). *Defining divorce adjustment: A study of marriage and family therapists' criteria for constructive long-term adjustment to divorce.* Unpublished doctoral dissertation, Purdue University, West Lafayette, IN.

Thomas, S.P. (1982). After divorce: Personality factors related to the process of adjustment. *Journal of Divorce, 5,* 19–36.

Thurnher, M., Fenn, C.B., Melichar, J., & Chiriboga, D.A. (1983). Sociodemographics: Perspectives on reasons for divorce. *Journal of Divorce, 6,* 25–35.

Walker, L. (1979). *The battered woman.* New York, NY: Harper & Row.

Wallerstein, J.S. (1986). Women after divorce: Preliminary report from a ten year follow-up. *American Journal of Orthopsychiatry, 56,* 65–77.

Wallerstein, J.S., & Kelly, J.B. (1980). *Surviving the breakup: How children and parents cope with divorce.* New York, NY: Basic Books.

Weingarten, H. (1988). The impact of late life divorce: A conceptual and empirical study. *Journal of Divorce, 12*(1), 21–39.

Weiss, R. (1975). *Marital separation.* New York, NY: Basic Books.

Weitzman, L.J. (1981). *The marriage contract: Spouses, lovers, and the law.* New York, NY: Free Press.

Weitzman, L.J. (1985). *The divorce revolution: The unexpected social and economic consequences for women and children in America.* New York, NY: Free Press.

Whisman, M.A., & Jacobson, N.S. (1989). Depression, marital satisfaction, and marital and personality measure of sex roles. *Journal of Marital and Family Therapy, 15*(2), 177–186.

Wortman, C. (1976). Causal attribution and personal control. In J.H. Harvey, W.J. Ickes, & R.F. Kidd (Eds.), *New directions in attribution research* (pp. 23–54). Hillsdale, NJ: Erlbaum.

Wortman, C. (1983). Coping and victimization: Conclusions and implications for future research. *Journal of Social Issues, 39*(2), 195–221.

Wright, C., & Maxwell, J. (1991). Social support during adjustment to later-life divorce: How adult children help parents. *Journal of Divorce & Remarriage, 15*(3/4), 21–48.

Zeiss, A.M., Zeiss, R.A., & Johnson, S.M. (1980). Sex differences in initiation of and adjustment to divorce. *Journal of Divorce, 4,* 22–33.

Zube, M. (1982). Changing behavior and outlook of aging men and women: Implications for marriage in the middle and later years. *Family Relations, 31,* 147–156.

■ ■ ■

2

Male Mid-Life Issues and Divorce

Sam Kirschner, PhD
Diana Adile Kirschner, PhD

The Man with Red Suspenders

John, a 40-year-old, successful insurance salesman, had been married for 20 years to Bev when the affair began. His paramour, Dorothy, was a 30-year-old blonde who was on a fast-track career path. She was, in complete contrast to his wife, Bev, attractive, highly verbal, and very passionate, both in bed and in the argumentative repartee that characterized her relationship with John. Bev, a 40-year-old housewife, had always been a steady, quiet, devoted mother and wife. She had created a very secure home environment with superb care for their three children. Over the course of 20 years, the couple had drifted apart. Bev had become more and more involved with her church group, whereas John had become more invested in his job. Bev had also slowly gained 50 pounds, whereas John had been playing racquetball regularly at the club. They rarely had sex.

John told Dorothy that he felt alive and young again with her, whereas at home he saw himself being "dead" and acting like an "old man." He began to dress more flamboyantly, wearing his new trademark, red trouser suspenders. He also got a hair transplant.

As the affair dragged on for 3 years, John wrestled with his guilt over being unfaithful to a "good" woman. When Bev finally found out about the relationship, she confronted John and then became quite depressed. The couple entered therapy to try to save the marriage, but treatment with two different therapists only revealed how empty their relationship had become. John finally divorced Bev and married Dorothy.

After 2 years of marriage, John again found himself unhappy because of the way Dorothy treated his children. He consulted the second author about his problems with Dorothy, and it was during these sessions that John talked about the affair and how his marriage had ended. When the therapist asked him what was the single biggest pressure in his life at the time of the onset of the affair, John replied that it was his work. The insurance company for which he had sold policies was in a severe decline. He was not able to advance at the company or to get another position elsewhere with matching compensation. He told the therapist that he had felt stagnant and stuck with no viable work alternatives. When he met Dorothy at work, he began to mentor her and his stagnation seemed to lift. The professional relationship had quickly blossomed into an affair by mutual desire.

The therapist pointed out to John that he had suffered from and was still undergoing a male mid-life crisis, which could lead to yet another divorce. John agreed that indeed he was worried that his inadequacies and immaturities would alienate Dorothy, and he contracted for ongoing individual and family therapy.

Dynamics of the Male Mid-Life Crisis

What are the dynamics of the male mid-life crisis, which at times, as in John's case, result in the fragmentation of family life or a divorce? Brim (1976) suggested that there are several major contributory factors to the mid-life crisis, including

- the measuring of one's achievements against ones hopes,
- recognition of one's mortality,
- changing relationships within the family,
- bodily changes,
- reworking of personal dreams,
- changes in status and role in the workplace, and
- overall issues of gcnerativity.

In addition, there are systemic variables that greatly affect men in mid-life. The major focus of this chapter, however, is on the individual, rather than on the system. We consider three important areas in men's lives: (a) work, (b) family/marriage, and (c) physical/personal issues.

Work

For most men, self-definition and self-image are closely tied to work. Therefore, how well they succeed in this area versus how much they had hoped to achieve is a very important issue in mid-life. A related variable is the evaluation of how well a man has provided for his family in terms of material success or standard of living versus his dreams and self-expectations. Indeed, generativity versus stagnation, the polarity that characterizes Erikson's (1950) seventh stage of ego development, which, in his schema, occurs at age 40, has much to do with productivity, creativity, and work-related issues.

Levinson (1978) pointed out that a man's generativity is often measured in his ability to mentor the next generation. In many instances, when this process does not take place with one's children, colleagues, or spouse, it can lead to an affair with a younger woman at work. The affair, in turn, can foment a marital crisis, which can either facilitate growth in the marriage or precipitate a divorce. In John's life, career dissatisfaction and feelings of stagnation had led to the need for a more rewarding experience at work. The mentoring relationship with Dorothy had rekindled his interest in work and improved his self-image.

Career success and satisfaction are clearly markers for many men in self-evaluations of personal progress. Yet, several studies have shown that career success and life satisfaction were not necessarily related to each other. For example, Aldous, Osmond, and Hicks (1979) found that men highest in occupational success were those with the least marital satisfaction. Similarly, Bray and Howard (1980) found that career success did not lead to personal happiness, but only to career satisfaction. In mid-life, this paradox of work success and personal unhappiness becomes painfully apparent to many men as they become more introspective and self-evaluative.

Family/Marriage

For many men, changes in family life are a critical factor in precipitating a mid-life crisis. As the children grow up and away from the family life, the empty nest forces a reevaluation of the marriage. In John's case, for example, the oldest child, a daughter, was in college, and the two younger ones were twin boys who were finishing high school. John enjoyed playing with his twins or watching sports on TV with them. When the twins were not around, he reported that it felt "empty in the house." In the context of the empty nest, John became painfully aware that his marriage had lost whatever sparkle it had once possessed, and that, for him, it was not worth saving.

When a man's sexual life at home is not satisfactory, he will, like John, often look outside the marriage for a sexual relationship that is fulfilling. Several studies have indicated that men's sexual interest in their spouses declines with age and that married women tend to attribute this decline to their husbands. Pfeiffer, Verwoerdt, and Davis (1972), echoing Kinsey, Pomeroy, Martin, and Gebhard (1953), also found that the men attributed the cessation of sexual relations with their partners to themselves. This loss of interest in mid-life can often spell the end of a marriage in cases in which men are sufficiently motivated to go outside the relationship to obtain satisfaction.

Physical/Personal Issues

Levinson (1978) identified the young/old polarity as a primary focus for the mid-life male. In his view, men in middle adulthood must find new ways of becoming either youthful or older. To do this, a man must let go of some aspects of being young, such as the ability to go without sleep or to perform athletically as he once had. On the other hand, a man must retain other qualities that can be reintegrated into his middle-aged self, such as seeking new challenges and experiences. A man needs to follow the same process regarding the qualities associated with being older. He must integrate attributes like perspective, self-awareness, and generosity into his identity so that these qualities can be fueled by the vital energies of his youthful side.

As Levinson pointed out, it is very difficult to maintain a harmonious balance between these two sides. Many men cling inappropriately to the juvenile and end up behaving immaturely. This can result in precipitous fragmentation of family life if the man becomes too self-centered and narcissistic.

The Zig-Zag Course of Human Development

Up to now, we have discussed the male mid-life crisis in terms of the specific pressures of this phase of the life cycle. However, although middle adulthood is unique in some ways, it also contains within it the unresolved polarities of prior epochs in a man's life. This is because human development occurs in a complex and rhythmic pattern, which is more a zig-zag rather than a straight line in which one stage is followed by another. In this pattern, adult evolution follows a dynamic flow of two modes: (a) the progressive and (b) the regressive. That is, adults have a tendency to move forward into new developmental areas, as well as backward to rework old unfinished business and unresolved issues from the past. In this way, they can constructively regress, progress again, and, in so doing, transform their lives (Kirschner & Kirschner, 1991).

This model of progress to regress to progress is reminiscent of Mahler's (1980) concept of rapprochement in the separation/individuation process of toddlers. Mahler observed that the very young child progresses out to explore new areas and new experiences of mastery, only to become self-conscious and regress once again to the arms of his or her mother. When the child is sufficiently reassured, he or she is ready to explore the world once again. We have noted that a similar oscillatory pattern appears throughout the life cycle and is not simply confined to the normal development of the child.

This cycle of progression followed by the experience of fears, doubts, separation anxiety, and a need for regressive contact with a rapprochement figure that in turn is followed by further progress in the world of mastery and doing has been called progressive abreactive regression (PAR; Stein, 1980). For a more complete description of the PAR process in individual and family development and its role in psychotherapy, the reader is referred to our text *Comprehensive Family Therapy* (Kirschner & Kirschner, 1986).

Mid-life represents a time of tremendous PAR in a mans life. On the progressive side, he has spent his adult years becoming successful at work, securing a home, and building a life-style and assets for the family. His children may have begun to leave the nest, and he must be ready to take his place as a grandfather and as an older person of the next generation. However, the movement forward also contains elements of decline and breakdown, which, in turn, lead to a regressive movement.

In mid-life, as the body begins to age, body image and youth become important concerns. Often a man at this age feels awkwardness and shame about his body, his balding, and his paunch. A man becomes very interested in proving his youth, virility, and attractiveness. Afraid of losing his sexuality, he seeks to enhance it. Young, attractive women often become the vehicles to confirm that his virility is intact. At the same time, however, he may also report fantasizing about the very sexy women he sees, a longing to approach them, coupled with a feeling of shyness and a fear of rejection.

This whole process is very similar to the process experienced by adolescent boys. As their bodies begin to change from prepubescence to a more mature, adult state, they become most concerned with their appearance and the issue of their attractiveness. They too feel as if they must prove themselves, especially in the area of virility. They will focus on gaining attention from the most attractive girls who may be in their environment in order to enhance their self-esteems. The bodily changes in mid-life, then, although in some ways opposite to those that occur in adolescence, bring up the same anxieties and self-doubts that remained unresolved from the earlier era.

Because of this similarity, the mid-life male has been called "middlescent" (Scarf, 1987). A number of other regressive processes that occur in mid-life involve the reworking of unresolved adolescent issues. There is a reworking of the destruction/creation polarity (Levinson, 1978). In both eras, there is a tendency to destroy the old: for the adolescent, the child identity; for the mid-life male, the old workaholic or staid provider identity. There is a tendency to seek the new and the exciting.

Perhaps most importantly, in mid-life, there is a strong separation/individuation issue, much like that in adolescence. As adolescents, many boys struggle with leaving home as part of the formation of their own personal identities. To become separate people, they must reject in part the attitudes and beliefs of their parents and embrace those of their peers. The separation process allows young adults to empower themselves and gain distance from their families. In time, this new perspective allows them to internalize and reintegrate admired or adaptive aspects of their parents' personalities and behavior.

Many men, however, have been unable to complete the separation/individuation process in adolescence and young adulthood. They may have experienced an engulfing, controlling parent, or parents who could not tolerate too much distance from the family. These young adults may have never really left home; they remain enmeshed in the family system; or, left with no other choice, they have cut off completely from their families. Other young adults grew up in families that can be characterized as very disengaged. In these systems, there were very loose and distant bonds between members. When the adolescents separated, no one really cared or noticed. These young men often will report feeling like lonely, lost boys who have no homes. They are then vulnerable to becoming seriously involved and married to women who are willing to "adopt" them.

All men have, to a certain degree, incomplete resolutions of separation/individuation in adolescence. To whatever degree the resolution is incomplete, it will arise in mid-life again as part of the PAR process. In particular, the marital relationships will be profoundly affected by the regressive forces of adolescence. This is because the spouse is like a transference figure; that is, she is endowed with the qualities and significance of a parent or authority. Throughout the marriage, the spouse has tended to enact specific roles vis-àvis her husband depending on his separation/individuation history. These roles include that of the engulfer, the rescuer, or the substitute mother. In each case, the role was initially a good fit for the man, based on his attachment/separation experiences from his family of origin.

Thus, in many marriages, the wives have played out a parental role with both their children and partner. To foster feelings of security and belongingness, many men have fused their identities with their wives/parents—a fusion that served as an emotional anchor when they were in the progressive, building phase. As they get older, however, and the PAR dynamic unfolds, they want to emerge, find themselves, and define themselves as separate and distinct from the fused marital/family unit.

As part of the abreactive process, some men become contrary, disagreeable, and less devoted to family duties. These men report that they are tired of being parents and husbands. They seek to detach from the intense bond they feel with their wives and to develop an autonomous "self." They are recapitulating the adolescent process of growing up and growing away. Often, such men feel engulfed and smothered, not only by their wives, but by their own parents or in-laws as well. In a belated adolescent gesture, they sometimes leave the family and cut off precipitously, because they feel that it is the only way they can leave.

Sometimes the separation issues are triggered by the wives. When the children begin to leave home, some women may return to school or may pursue careers. The husbands who were secure when they were in the lead, promoting change in family life, can become quite anxious when their partners take on new roles. These men, like adolescents, feel threatened and abandoned when their "motherly" wives shift focus away from them and the family. Although they have outwardly prided themselves on their strength and independence, especially at work, they have unknowingly relied on the secure emotional base of their wives at home. This is similar to adolescents who are cavalier about "not needing their parents" and yet fall apart if one of them becomes sick or separates from the family.

Many men, however, are able to successfully navigate the internal storms of mid-life. They use the regression to adolescence constructively to rediscover their vitality and some of their lost dreams. With their new energies, they are able to actualize some of these dreams in middle and later adulthood while maintaining the stability of married life. For these men, the progress to regress to progress cycle leaves them better prepared to cope with the stresses of illness, aging, and ultimately the loss of their spouses or their own deaths.

Growth Versus Divorce

Why do the adolescent issues that erupt in mid-life lead to divorce in some cases, whereas in others they seem to propel the marriage to a new level? We theorize that the keys lie in the amount of adaptability that is available in the marriage, and in the way in which the wives resolve their own mid-life crises. Olson, Sprenkle, and Russell (1979) postulated that healthy couples are characterized by both cohesion and adaptability. Couples who have made it to mid-life typically have a good deal of cohesiveness. However, they may lack the ability to adapt to the powerful PAR forces that are at work in this stage. In healthier couples, the spouses can grow and accommodate to the pressures and adolescent-like demands. For example, in one case, the wife responded to her husband's affair by rediscovering her own sexuality, and redefined herself in terms of her own constructive narcissism and attractiveness. She then stepped out of the mother role and into the role of the "new" lover. In therapy, she was able to get in touch with her own anger so that the couple could first air and then negotiate their differences. As a result, the spouses learned how to support each other in the pursuit of unique interests and talents. Their relationship adapted so that it could support individuation without the marriage fragmenting.

On the other hand, John was ill prepared to cope with the PAR forces that had been unleashed, and his marriage lacked adaptability. He was unaware of the mid-life dynamics that were shaping his life until after he entered couples therapy with his new wife. Rather, he experienced that his affair with Dorothy just "seemed to happen." This lack of awareness is also typical in the beginning of this type of mid-life crisis. John, like other men, was just emerging from the progressive cycle in which he was almost totally absorbed in his work. He had not been at all attentive to his own inner process, and had unconsciously acted out the regressive aspects of his adolescence.

John's evolution led to divorce because his first marriage was not one in which there was a high degree of adaptability. In this relationship, Bev was not able to develop herself in ways that would complement John's growth. John had asked Bev to lose weight and wear sexy clothes for him. Initially, she refused, maintaining that true love meant that John should accept her unconditionally. This was impossible for John to do because he was on a path of transforming himself in the direction of youth, sexuality, and vitality. As the marriage unraveled, Bev made some attempts to change, but her attempts were negatively reinforced by John, who reported that he just couldn't see Bev as thin or sexy. John was projecting the matronly, old, and unattractive aspects of his own mother onto Bev. She then would unconsciously get back into her old marital role and give up her own development. The marital system, then, could not accommodate or adapt to John's mid-life transformation.

● ● ●

Because the issues of mid-life have been well documented, there are a number of clear implications for treatment. Whenever a mid-life male or his spouse consults for therapy, the therapist will be dealing with complex individual and marital issues that affect the personal evolution of both spouses and marriage. Thus, unless divorce is the client's clear-cut goal, individual sessions with each spouse as well as couples sessions would be indicated.

Individual work with the mid-life male would help him to rework his adolescent-like dilemmas regarding youth and generativity, along with relational and separation/individuation needs. Individual work with his spouse would be focused on educating her about some of these themes and polarities, as well as working on her own mid-life issues. Couples sessions are needed to help the spouses take back their own projections and to transform the negatively reinforcing patterns of communication that characterize the marital system. We have found that the combination of individual and conjoint sessions with mid-life men and their spouses has been effective in supporting the individual growth of the man while maintaining the integrity of the marriage (Kirschner & Kirschner, 1986). In order to work coherently with all aspects of the individual/marital/family system, these sessions are ideally conducted by a single practitioner. In this way, the myriad and complex issues of the adult/couple at mid-life can be worked with synergistically with maximum efficiency—in a way that promotes both cohesiveness and adaptability.

References

Aldous, J., Osmond, M., & Hicks, M.W. (1979). Men's work and men's families. In W.R. Burr (Ed.), *Contemporary theories about the family* (pp. 227–256). New York, NY: Free Press.

Bray, D., & Howard, A. (1980). Career success and life satisfactions of middle-aged managers. In L. Bond & J. Rosen (Eds.), *Competence and coping* (pp. 258–287). Hanover, NH: University Press of New England.

Brim, O.G. (1976). Theories of the male mid-life crisis. *Counseling Psychologist, 6,* 2–9.

Erikson, E. (1950). *Childhood and society.* New York, NY: W.W. Norton.

Kinsey, A.C., Pomeroy, W.B., Martin, C.E., & Gebhard, P. (1953). *Sexual behavior in the human female.* Philadelphia, PA: W.B. Saunders.

Kirschner, D.A., & Kirschner, S. (1986). *Comprehensive family therapy: An integration of systemic and psychodynamic treatment models.* New York, NY: Brunner/Mazel.

Kirschner, S., & Kirschner, D.A. (1991). The two faces of change: Progression and regression. In R.C. Curtis & G. Stricker (Eds.), *How people change* (pp. 117–127). New York, NY: Plenum Press.

Levinson, D.J. (1978). *The seasons of a man's life.* New York, NY: Ballantine.

Mahler, M. (1980). On the first three subphases of the separation-individuation process. *International Journal of Psychoanalysis, 53,* 333–338.

Olson, D.H., Sprenkle, D., & Russell, C. (1979). Circumplex model of marital and family systems: I. Cohesion and adaptability dimensions, family types and clinical application. *Family Process, 18,* 3–37.

Pfeiffer, E., Verwoerdt, A., & Davis, G.C. (1972). Sexual behavior in middle life. *American Journal of Psychiatry, 128,* 82–87.

Scarf, M. (1987). *Intimate partners.* New York, NY: Random House.

Stein, A. (1980). Comprehensive family therapy. In R. Herink (Ed.), *The psychotherapy handbook.* New York, NY: New American Library.

■ ■ ■

3

Divorce and Health in Later Life

Charles B. Hennon, PhD
Timothy H. Brubaker, PhD

D ivorce can be conceptualized as a meaningful life experience or event that influences an individual in several ways (Baum, 1988; Hagestad & Smyer, 1982; Moen & Howery, 1988). Divorce is an experience that is used to make sense of one's existence, the timing of which is related to other aspects of one's life course, has the potential to alter behavior and produce stress, may result in decreased emotional or mental health functioning, and/or produces more vulnerability to pathophysiological processes. No matter at what age divorce occurs, it has the potential of affecting one's health in later life. Utilizing stress theory as an organizing framework, this chapter reviews research on divorce and health in the middle and later years. A contextual stress model is developed that can help interventionists better understand how divorce and health may be related in later life. With this knowledge, professionals may be able to better tailor their clinical strategies.

The chapter is organized as follows. First, limitations to current understanding of the relationship between divorce and health in later life are outlined, and then the theoretical linkage between stress and health will be reviewed. The prevalence of and trends in incidence of being divorced and divorcing in later life are next reviewed. The literature review is organized by type of health—first physical and then mental. A contextual stress model of the theoretical linkage among variables that may influence the relationship between health status and divorce in later life is then used to integrate the research findings. The chapter ends by noting that interventionists should keep abreast of research on cohorts as well as developmental explanations of the relationships between divorce and health in later life.

Limitation to the Understanding of any Relationship between Divorce and Health in Later Life

Research on divorce and the divorce process for those in later life is sparse (Brubaker, 1990a). Additionally, there are several issues that might plague clear understanding of any observed relationship among life stage, divorce, and health. First, the relationship may be spurious in the sense that it is not divorce per se that is the causal agent, but related hardships (economic, loss of social support, etc.) that place the person at risk for poor health. Second, the relationship may also be confounded in the sense that some divorced persons engage in behaviors or practices (i.e., life-styles) that place them at greater risk (poorer nutrition, more carousing, etc.; Ross, 1991). Third, the short-run costs and benefits of divorce may be quite different from the long-term consequences (Brubaker & Hennon, 1992). Fourth, the age at which a person divorces (age at decree) may be during a different life stage than his or her current one; thus, effects related to divorcing (process) in later life may be different from effects related to being divorced (marital status) in later life (Brubaker, 1985).

Fifth, the pathways, mechanisms, and consequences of divorcing and the adjustment or adaptational outcomes (somatic, emotional, social) to divorce may vary by gender, socioeconomic status, length of time separated, initiator of the divorce, or other important categorical variables. These categorical factors may be important in understanding the process of divorce and its effect on health. However, the studies reviewed here have not consistently examined differences by such categories. Sixth, the health status reported in an empirical study of the relationship between divorce and health may well have preceded the marital status, and could have been a causal factor of the divorce (Fenwick & Barresi, 1981; Gove, Style, & Hughes, 1990). Seventh, the mechanisms and pathways may differ for physical and mental health. Eighth, the seriousness of the disorders observed, acute or chronic status, and their prevalence may differ by gender, and also be affected by factors that covary with gender and divorce, such as economic status or child custody (Keith, 1986a, 1986b, 1989b).

A ninth issue is related to the indicators of health or morbidity. Some indicators (i.e., days in bed) are perhaps more an indication of illness behavior as opposed to morbidity per se, and thus are not completely determined by actual level of morbidity (Mechanic, 1974). The newly separated or divorced may have limited ability to respond to real or perceived problems by resting in bed. They may have to forego this option to fulfill the tasks of everyday life that could perhaps be carried out by a spouse (Fenwick & Barresi, 1981). Likewise, self-reported morbidity or emotional health may not always correlate highly with other measures of these same phenomena. Another potential confounding variable is the use of global (e.g., health status) versus more specific (e.g., coronary disease) morbidity indicators or causes of death, and also whether researchers consider the severity (well-being or depression, colds or cancer) of the ailments.

Few, if any, studies have adequately controlled for all or even most of these factors. Thus, the few data on later life divorce and health should be cautiously interpreted. There is a need for more sophisticated analyses that control for confounding variables. For example, the use of longitudinal designs and time-series analysis is necessary, and more emphasis placed on gender and different types of divorcing processes (including desirability of the divorce and time divorced) would enhance the research. Nonetheless, the current database of empirical analyses provide some information for a cautious review.

Stress and Health

It is well known that a link has been perceived between stressful life events and disease (Holmes & Rahe, 1967; Moen & Howery, 1988), and also, more specifically, between divorce and morbidity, both physical and mental (Gove et al., 1990; Himmelfarb, 1984). However, the evidence for this link has been somewhat tenuous (Newberry, Baldwin, Madden, & Gerstenberger, 1987; Rose & Levin, 1979). Although some research has shown a relationship between stress and morbidity, other research has indicated this relationship to be weak; that is, stress may have greater effects on those already predisposed to disease (Newberry et al., 1987). Several authors have pointed out that the conceptualization of both stress and disease is rather messy (Moen & Howery, 1988; Rose & Levin, 1979). Thus, although the stress concept and stress process are being used to help organize this chapter, it is recognized that this relationship may be more perceived than real and that more research is needed to empirically establish the link between stressful life events and various health outcomes. Specifically, the linkages between divorce and health status among middle-aged and older individuals must be further specified.

Exact definitions of stress have been hard to establish, especially because researchers have used different models (e.g., medical, psychological, or behavioral) in their studies (Newberry et al., 1987). For the purposes of reviewing the literature for this chapter and providing guidelines for interpretation and discussion of results, a definition of stress that emphasizes person–environment relationships was used. Stress has been conceptualized as a response made by an individual relative to demands from his or her environment. This model is cognitive-phenomenological in that a person must perceive a demand and experience some tension to respond (Coyne & Lazarus, 1980). An individual's coping or management strategy can include cognitive and behavioral responses, as well as direct action oriented to change the stressor, to control the felt stress, or to cognitively construct the situation in a way that it is perceived as less stressful (Coyne & Lazarus, 1980). Management strategies can prove to be more or less functional or dysfunctional. Thus, they can have positive or negative consequences in either or both the short or long term. Adaptational outcomes can be at the somatic, emotional (morale or mental), or social levels (Coyne & Lazarus, 1980).

This conceptualization is improved by situating it within contextual understanding. The contextual frame emphasizes the context within which the individual or family behavior occurs (Brubaker, 1990b; Brubaker & Brubaker, 1992a). This contextual approach embodies two different pathways between stress and health outcomes: (a) external loops and (b) internal loops (Newberry et al., 1987). Basically, external loop models suggest that the relationship between stressors and health outcomes is due to behavioral changes of the individual. That is, as a result of the various demands perceived and their appraisals, individuals act in ways that place them at risk for poor health. For example, persons undergoing divorce may respond in such ways that their behavior places them at risk (Umberson, 1987). They may have a poorer diet, smoke more, drink more, and be exposed to various infectious diseases because of their interactions with more and different people.

Internal loop models argue that health outcomes are more a direct result of stress. Basically these models suggest that stress has an effect on the immune and other systems, and thus people become more susceptible to a variety of ill-health outcomes; thus, it may be argued that stress directly causes illness in some way (Rose & Levin, 1979). It can be assumed that people become more susceptible to cardiovascular disease, cancer, or other kinds of outcomes due to the various physical responses to the stress of divorce.

A definitive link between stress and disease is beyond the scope of this chapter. However, a closer identification of the context of divorce or divorcing in the middle and later years can be made. The primary question is: How is divorce as a stressor related to the health of middle-aged and older persons?

Demographics of Divorce in Later Life

Divorce is one of the demographic developments that has been influencing family relationships and the quality of life for older persons (Bengtson, 1986; Uhlenberg & Myers, 1981). Besides divorcing during later life, people can move into this period of life either single from an earlier divorce (or divorces; Glick, 1984) or remarried after divorce. Schoen, Urton, Woodrow, and Baj (1985) reported that for the 1908 to 1927 birth cohorts, the proportion of marriages ending in divorce is between 24% to 32%. The average age at divorce for these cohorts of men has been reported as approximately 40 years compared with about 37 years for women. The estimated proportion of these people remarrying is between 75% and 82%. The incidence of separation and divorce is still relatively low among the older U.S. population (Brubaker & Hennon, 1992). Basically, once a person has reached middle age, there is a lower risk of becoming separated or divorced than when in a younger age group.

The proportion of those divorced among the older U.S. population (ages 65 years and over) more than doubled between 1960 and 1979 (Uhlenberg & Myers, 1981). Bengtson (1986) noted that each year in the United States, over 10,000 people over the age of 65 experience divorce. Uhlenberg and Myers projected that between the years 2010 and 2020, approximately one third to over half of middle-aged and older people will have been divorced at least once. Hess and Waring (1983) projected that the proportion of divorced and never remarried women who reach old age is expected to greatly increase in the future. Martin and Bumpass (1989) estimated that 64% of marriages will be disrupted (separation and/or divorce) by 40 years after marriage, and Preston (1984) pointed out that a greater percentage of men remarry at least one time. Further, Glick (1984) suggested that many people will become redivorced before or after reaching old age.

Although older people have been at lower risk, this risk has been rising. The most recent statistics (National Center for Health Statistics, 1991) have shown that the divorce rates for men in later life varied from 17.0 (ages 45–49 years) to 1.9 (ages 65 years and over) and from 13.0 (ages 45–49 years) to 1.5 (ages 65 years and over) for women. All age-specific divorce rates for older men and women, except for men ages 65 years and over, were higher in 1988 than in 1970. Conversely, divorce rates for those most at risk (ages 25–39 years for men and ages 20–39 years for women) declined between 1980 and 1988. (Some of the data discussed in this chapter are available in tabular form from the authors, or see Brubaker & Hennon, 1992.)

The number of people ages 45 years and over who divorce each year has been increasing since 1980. We have calculated that 103,530 men ages 45 years and over divorced in 1988, compared with 83,340 in 1980. For women, the comparable numbers are 71,226 and 57,228. Thus, in 1988, 174,756 people in the United States were ages 45 years or over when their divorce decrees became final. This represented 19.9% of all divorces among men that year and 13.7% among women. It should be noted that these are not necessarily dissolutions of first marriages.

The mean age at divorce in 1988 was 36.9 and 34.4 years for men and women, respectively. For second marriages, it was 41.5 years for men and 38.2 years for women. Among all remarriages, the mean age at divorce for men was 42.5 years, and it was 39.0 years for women. The proportion of divorces granted to couples married 20 years or longer has been increasing. In 1988, of all divorces granted, about 12% went to couples married 20 years or longer (National Center for Health Statistics, 1991).

Recently, the probability of remarrying has decreased (Glick, 1989). Although the rate of divorce increased during the 1970s, the rate for remarriage among divorced persons decreased sharply, and during the 1980s it decreased moderately (Glick, 1989; Norton & Moorman, 1987).

Given recent divorce trends for all age groups, the reduction in remarriage rates, and the fact that remarriages are more prone to disruption than first marriages (Martin & Bumpass, 1989), it can be expected that increasing proportions of both men and women will be living divorced in later life (Uhlenberg & Myers, 1981). This may be particularly true for women because the remarriage rates for men have tended to be higher than for women (Glick, 1984; Schoen et al., 1985). Also, the realities of different proportions of each gender surviving until later ages has made it less likely for a woman to remarry in later life. Thus, it is possible that a woman divorcing at any age is more likely to be single during the later years of her life than is a man (Norton & Moorman, 1987).

Some scholars have noted that those people who enter later life as currently married individuals are less at risk for poor health consequences (Gove, 1972). It has not become clear from previous research whether remarried people are more similar to married or divorced individuals in terms of health status and other quality of life variables. That is, the remarried individual may or may not be like a long-term married person in terms of general levels of well-being or other outcome factors that have been associated with the status of being married (Bulcroft, Bulcroft, Hatch, & Borgatta, 1989). A key question is: Does divorce result in nonreversible effects on health, or does remarriage negate the effects? If the latter part of this question is supported, and Gove and his colleagues (1990) seemed to have done so, it would appear that it is not the stress of divorce per se that is harmful to health, but rather something about the status of being divorced (such as living alone) that is harmful. Katschke-Jennings and Healy (1987) suggested, for example, that although remarriage could be stressful in its own way, it could also be a mechanism to provide special joys like companionship, intimacy, and caregiving, thus altering the divorced person's living context. As Menaghan and Lieberman (1986) stated, the emphasis on changing marital status has created an unprecedented fluidity in marital status. Thus, for many later life people, the status of married, divorced, and remarried may be fleeting. Therefore, the effect of changing versus not changing marital status on the health of later life individuals may be important to investigate.

Physical Health and Divorce

It has been well established that as people age they become more at risk for many illnesses and disabilities. It has also been noted (Aldous, 1987) that the health of the elderly has been improving. As more people have been reaching the later stages of life, they have tended to do so in better health. Frail elderly have become common only in the more advanced age categories (75 years and older). However, the mechanisms explaining the relationships between marital status and health over the life course and how those affect health in later life are not well understood. An underlying assumption guiding much of the research concerning this relationship is that divorce is stressful and thus has implications for health (Ahrons, 1983; Haring-Hidore, Stock, Okun, & Witter, 1985).

In general, married individuals including those in later life have appeared to be at an advantage relative to overall health status (Gove et al., 1990; Lee, Seccombe, & Shehan, 1991; Zick & Smith, 1991). Several studies have indicated that married people (especially husbands) have been healthier and have used medical services less than have divorced, separated, single, or widowed individuals (especially men), and that the divorced and separated have experienced more acute conditions and more limiting chronic conditions (see, e.g., Brubaker & Hennon, 1992; Chiriboga, 1982; Fenwick & Barresi, 1981; Gove, 1972; Gove et al., 1990; Guarnaccia, Angel, & Worobey, 1991; House, Landis, & Umberson, 1988; Keith & Lorenz, 1989; Lee et al., 1991; McKinley, McKinley, & Brambilla, 1987; Verbrugge, 1979, 1983; Zick & Smith, 1991). According to Holmes and Rahe (1967), divorce has ranked second and marital separation has ranked third in affecting the health of individuals. Although little research has specifically investigated middle-aged or older cohorts, it is generally expected that the relationships that have been revealed among marital status, morbidity, and mortality apply to persons of all ages. The evidence for these relationships has mostly been based on correlational data, and it is not necessarily correct to assume that health status has been a result of, or that it even has developed after, a transition into the current marital status. It is proposed here that health problems are sometimes related to marital problems, and marital problems are then related to becoming divorced.

Chiriboga (1982) and Menaghan and Lieberman (1986) reported that older women experience an improvement in physical health after divorce and that this may be due to the release they feel after exiting confining marriages. They also noted that men are relatively unaware of marital problems that precede divorce, whereas women are likely to see the predivorce period of life as excruciating. Older men have been reported as showing less improvement in physical health after divorce relative to women, as well as being less happy and more troubled. If life strains are sustained, they may support the development of a sense of demoralization, stress, and, consequently, illness, disability, or higher mortality later in life (Keith & Lorenz, 1989; Zick & Smith, 1991).

The observed relationship between divorce and ill health outcomes may be due to a variety of internal or external individual stress factors (sometimes referred to as internal or external loop pathways). It may be that once people have begun the divorcing process, they have often exposed themselves through risk-taking behavior to poor health outcomes. The currently reported health status may also have been because of other life changes, such as in employment, lack of financial ability to seek medical assistance, loss of insurance benefits, and normal transitions associated with the family life cycle or life course (Brubaker & Hennon, 1992). Health has perhaps been affected by fairly direct effects on the immune or other bodily systems due to stress of divorce as a life event (Mikhail, 1981; Selye, 1980). Whatever the reason, it seems clear that although some older people (especially women) may experience an improvement in physical health, people who are currently divorced are at a higher risk for poor health than are those who are currently married.

Mental Health and Divorce

Studies that have analyzed the relationship between marital status and well-being have generally concluded that those who are divorced report less psychological well-being than those who are married (Glenn & Weaver, 1988; Gove et al., 1990; Haring-Hidore et al., 1985; Kessler & Essex, 1982; Lee et al., 1991; Menaghan & Lieberman, 1986; Williams, 1988). However, the magnitude of the association is perhaps not as strong as has been suggested, particularly so in the research done with older samples (Haring-Hidore et al., 1985). The association may also be spurious or due to selection factors related to who marries or divorces (Glenn & Weaver, 1988; Williams, 1988). In addition, gender appears to play a factor (Kessler & McRae, 1984).

Compared with men, middle-aged women experience higher amounts of depression and other mental illnesses (Kessler & McRae, 1984; McKinley et al., 1987; Thoits, 1986), and it has also been suggested that marital status seems to be more related to health status among women compared with men. Men seem to benefit more from marriage (Verbrugge, 1979; Williams, 1988). However, some have argued that there may be a gender-specific selection factor relative to mental health and marriage. That is, men who are mentally unhealthy are selected out of marriage, whereas women who are mentally unhealthy are selected into marriage (Gove et al., 1990; Kessler & McRae, 1984). Relative to the relationship between marital status and well-being, it has been argued that the "happiness gap" is an effect of marriage rather than related to selection factors (Lee et al., 1991; Williams, 1988).

Institutionalization has been suggested as "a clear indicator of a person's ability to function effectively and appropriately and serves as a general indicator of one's mental and physical well-being" (Gove et al., 1990, p. 8). Married individuals have had the lowest rates of institutionalization. Among the 45–65 year age group, both males and females (but especially males) have been much more likely to be in mental institutions if they were divorced (or never married) than if they were married (or widowed; Gove et al., 1990). A similar pattern has held for younger persons. There has perhaps been some bias in treatment by marital status. Many separated and divorced women have lived with children, and these child-care responsibilities could have deterred women from seeking psychiatric hospitalization. This could have produced an artificially low rate in the treatment data.

Menaghan and Lieberman (1986) argued that people can gain from a divorce. That is, although the divorced are worse off in terms of well-being when they have been compared with all married people, when compared with unhappily married people, the divorced have higher morale and fewer symptoms of depression. Gove and his colleagues (1990) pointed out that "it is not marriage per se that produces a positive state of well-being" (p. 14), but rather the quality of the relationship. House and Robbins (1983) indicated that persistent marital strife is more deleterious to mental health than the singular life event of divorce. Renne (1971) concluded that depression is a consequence of unhappy marriage rather than of divorce. Other studies have also indicated that people have improved in well-being after a divorce.

McCullough and Zick (1992) noted that women heading single-parent homes believe they are making better progress toward reaching their life goals, relative to full-time homemakers. Ross (1991) theorized that marriage can decrease a woman's sense of control, mastery, personal efficacy, or personal autonomy. Although divorced men have been shown to have a higher sense of control than married men, overall it has appeared that married women give up more of their independence than do married men. Several studies (Menaghan & Lieberman, 1986) have suggested that divorced women have sometimes enjoyed autonomy and freedom from the conflicts they had when married. It has been argued, then, that the more distressed the person has been in a marriage, the more the potential gain that can be experienced through a divorce. Kessler and McRae (1984) and Gove (1972) noted that the relative mental health of separated and divorced women has been better than that of married women, a pattern opposite to that which has been observed in men.

The causes of female mental illness cannot be looked for exclusively within the stressors and strains of marriage. Thoits (1986) noted that the "risk of distress" may be higher for women compared with men regardless of marital status, and Kessler and McRae (1984) noted that women exceed men in emotional stress among the never married and previously married, as well as among the married. However, the relative mental health of women versus men has been worse among the married than among those of other marital statuses. Although Fox (1980) noted that the distress of unmarried (including divorced) women has exceeded that of unmarried men, this difference was smaller than the differences among married persons.

Older women have been reported to have more difficulty in adjusting to divorce than older men (Farnsworth, Pett, & Lund, 1989). They specifically have indicated more helplessness, avoidance, anger, guilt, and confusion. These factors have been seen as related to older divorced women having more difficulty in managing loss. Himmelfarb (1984), on the other hand, reported data showing that among older people, only married and widowed women reported higher levels of poor mental health symptoms than did men of similar marital statuses. Thus, divorced older men and women have seemed to be similar in mental health status in at least one study.

Chiriboga, Roberts, and Stein (1978) noted a higher level of depression among divorced men relative to divorced women, and Chiriboga (1982) noted that divorcing women reported more psychological symptoms and emotional tension than men. Across age groups, those in their 40s averaged the fewest symptoms, and those ages 50 years and over averaged the most. An explanation that has been given for these findings is that older divorced people have difficulty detaching from the former life-style, perceive fewer options for the future, and have a general uncertainty about what to do next. Both the process and the status of divorce are thus stressful, and this is manifested in various symptoms of mental (and physical) illness.

Given the somewhat mixed results reported relative to the association of divorce with mental health status and how this relationship might vary with gender and age, it might be hypothesized that the mixture of stressors associated with divorcing (including the pile-up of demands; McCubbin & Patterson, 1983), combined with the stress management abilities of individuals and their other resources, are causal factors in explaining the mental health adaptational outcomes related with later life divorce. If variations exist (either individual differences or across categories of people, such as gender) in stress management abilities or coping resources available, then poorer mental health may result. However, it appears clear from the results reported in the literature that divorce per se cannot be considered such a major life event that mental or emotional health is affected directly through internal processes. Rather, further elaboration and specification are necessary to identify what aspects of persons' external contexts in concert with their personal stress management abilities are responsible for observed mental health statuses.

McKinley and associates (1987) pointed out that there is a variety of caregiver roles played by women, especially for ailing husbands and aging parents, and this has been a major potential source of depression. As women have taken on these roles (Brody, 1990; Hennon, Brubaker, & Kaplan, 1991), particularly as they and their husbands aged and as parents survived into even later life with chronic disabilities, it has become more likely that women will become depressed. However, it may be hypothesized that as more women become divorced, they collectively will be taking on less of a caregiver role for their husbands and in-laws. Thus, as more women become divorced, it is possible that fewer women will become depressed because playing family roles is related to depression among middle-age women (Himmelfarb, 1984). The lack of intensity in these roles after divorce might explain the better mental health of divorced and separated later life women that has been reported by some investigators.

It has been well documented that depression, psychological disorders, and other emotional or somatic morbidity have been associated with lower socioeconomic status, and it has been shown that women's socioeconomic status has tended to decrease after divorce (Brubaker & Hennon, 1992; McKinley et al., 1987; Morgan, 1991; Voydanoff, 1990; Weitzman, 1985; Zick & Smith, 1991). Thus, such factors as amount of education and employment appear to also be aspects of individuals' contexts that can buffer the potential effects of divorce on individuals in later life (Brubaker & Hennon, 1992). Also, some people are better equipped to manage loss and/or develop strategies against stressors or strains. In addition, the accumulation of roles and consequent role strain and conflict appear to relate to depression (Thoits, 1986).

Although divorce may reduce tension, this explanation seems, given the empirical findings, to explain relationships between marital status and health for later life women better than for later life men. Although good emotional health may sometimes be a positive adaptational outcome of using divorce as a way to cope with the stresses of marriage, adaptations on other levels (e.g., somatic) may be less positive. Although divorce may be seen as functional coping in some ways, it may be a dysfunctional coping technique in other ways for the stresses associated with marriage. As it has been noted, seeing situations as positive and feeling in control (mastery) appear to be related to better well-being and less distress (Coyne & Lazarus,

1980). Those seeking divorce and/or seeing it as a positive alternative within their contexts might experience less emotional symptomatology than those not seeking divorce and/or those appraising it in less positive ways (Keith, 1986b; Kincaid & Caldwell, 1991). Also, one's original coping behavior can have the effect of producing stress at a later point in time, or becoming a stressor in its own right. Thus, although the emotional or mental health reactions associated with divorcing may be positive at one point in time, the process itself or resulting conditions (e.g., financial) may prove to be stress producing and thus potentially harmful to good health in a longer time period.

It appears that the research does not support an internal loop pathway (e.g., that divorce itself creates stress that affects health directly) between divorce and poor mental health among later life individuals. Rather, it would seem that a variety of potential coping resources and stress management strategies affect adaptational outcomes, and thus provide evidence for more of an external loop explanation. That is, individuals who are divorced are differently able to allocate resources to help them manage the demands of divorce, as well as how they appraise and reappraise (Coyne & Lazarus, 1980) their situations. The contexts within which individuals' resources are allocated are an important consideration.

Context, Stress, and Health

It has been reported that virtually all data indicate that the married have higher levels of well-being than the unmarried (Gove et al., 1990). This relationship between marital status and health appears to be particularly strong for psychological well-being. Married persons have also been shown to have a substantially lower mortality rate, but with the differences among rates across marital statuses being smaller in the later years of life. The divorced and separated have seemed to experience more acute conditions and more limiting chronic conditions. Among the noninstitutionalized unmarried population, the divorced and separated have been documented as being the least healthy; the next least healthy being widows and the never married (Mergenhagen, Lee, & Gove, 1985; Verbrugge, 1979). However, some recent data suggest that although this is still true among the divorced elderly, in younger age groups including middle-aged (45–64 years of age), other unmarried statuses appear to be more at risk for mortality. The strength of the association between marital status and health status may be weakening, and it appears that the divorced as a group have lately become more healthy relative to their married counterparts (Mergenhagen et al., 1985).

Some authors have suggested that the health problems (especially mental) of those who have undergone marital status changes (especially divorce events) have been a causal factor in the change, rather than being a consequence of the change (Fenwick & Barresi, 1981). On the other hand, Fenwick and Barresi (1981) and others (see Gove et al., 1990; Zick & Smith, 1991) provided longitudinal data that suggest that marital status changes among the elderly have been prior to, and thus a causal factor in, health status change. Fenwick and Barresi's data also have been interpreted to show that marital status differences and changes have been more important in explaining health status of the elderly than the characteristics of age, race, education, and gender. Fenwick and Barresi suggested that their analysis adds weight to the argument that it is not change per se that is stressful, but the desirability of that change. However, they failed to control for desirability through determining the subjective appraisal of their respondents. That is, they seemed to have considered that their subjects perceived their divorces as undesirable.

Another factor to consider is that the over-64 years of age cohort reached adulthood at a time when divorce was not normative, and when becoming unmarried (and remaining unmarried) was viewed as a failure or due to personality or physical deficits. Members of this cohort may feel a great deal of strain due to this negative status (Katschke-Jennings & Healy, 1987; Keith, 1986a; Mergenhagen et al., 1985). This stigma and response could have had an effect on physical and mental health. As Keith (1986a) pointed out, the limited research on older divorced persons has suggested that they have been especially vulnerable to both physical and mental health problems, higher mortality rates, and lower life satisfaction.

With these two factors (timing of divorce relative to health status, social stigma of divorce) in mind, attention is now turned to integrating the literature on divorce and health in later life. To do so, a contextual stress framework is utilized. Two variables, economic context and social context, are considered; then the relationships between context and health, and stress and health, are considered for later life divorced persons.

Economic Context

Cross-sectional studies have seemed to suggest that life change events and economic deprivation have a negative effect on the health of older people (Fenwick & Barresi, 1981). In fact, one of the more negative consequences of lower socioeconomic status has been poor health among the elderly (Keith & Lorenz, 1989). Keith and Lorenz reported a significant relationship between age and the financial strain of divorced and separated persons. Those who were relatively younger were more affected by marital dissolution (average age of sample was 60.5 years). However, these researchers found no relationship between financial strain and worsened health among formerly married older people. This may mean that these people have had excellent stress management skills.

Keith (1985) and Hennon (1983) provided evidence that divorced later life persons have a suppressed economic well-being. Women have appeared to be more deprived and vulnerable after divorce than men (Morgan, 1991; Pett & Vaughan-Cole, 1986; Weitzman, 1985). Hess and Waring (1983) went as far as to suggest that the financial, health, and emotional statuses of divorced older women are extremely precarious. If divorce has occurred earlier in life, the deficits from inadequate or no property settlement, lack of alimony payments, or responsibility for support of children, and perhaps also reduced labor force participation, may have had a cumulative effect of limiting financial security for women in old age, as well as probably affecting physical and mental health (Keith, 1985). It also has been suggested that an immediate economic impact of separation or divorce for older women may have included ineligibility to share pension or health benefits with their former spouses (Keith, 1985). However, it should be noted that the financial resources of older men may also have been diminished due to their maintenance of separate households, alimony payments (even if for a short time period), loss of assets such as housing, and other economic consequences of divorce including perhaps even discrimination in the labor market (DeShane & Brown-Wilson, 1981).

Hyman (1983) and Hennon (1983) found that older divorced and separated persons, especially men, were less satisfied with their financial situations (relative to widowed and married). Even though divorced men may objectively be financially better off than divorced women, divorced men have been more likely to offer negative evaluations of their financial status (Keith, 1985). It has been suggested that among older persons with lower incomes, the loss of a spouse (by death or dissolution of the marriage) has been associated with poor health over any time period. One longitudinal study (Fenwick & Barresi, 1981) found that those elderly who had a lower income and lost a spouse, regardless of when the loss had occurred, had lower levels of health than did the married or the never married. The evidence shows a relationship between divorce, economic status, and health among those in later life. Thus, to understand the relationship between divorce, stress, and health, the economic context must be examined.

Social Context

Another explanation of the relationship between health and divorce in later life is a lack of support systems or care providers (Brubaker & Hennon, 1992; House et al., 1988). That is, those who have been divorced and particularly those who have been living by themselves may have less social support (Uhlenberg & Myers, 1981; Zick & Smith, 1991), and this is related to risk-taking behavior, lacking a significant other to validate one's self, poor emotional well-being, poor mental health, and thus poor physical health (Brubaker & Hennon, 1992; Gove et al., 1990). Without a caregiver in the home, people may be more at risk due to factors such as poor dietary practices or the lack of primary health care or prevention. Also, especially for fathers, relationships with children may suffer after divorce; thus, this potential source of social support may be weak or lacking in later life.

Older people have been shown to benefit through a social support system of caregivers and people who provide emotional support. It also has been discovered that the number of older people living with a relative has decreased over the last few decades, but the amount of contact has not necessarily decreased (Keith, 1986a). This has been partly due to improved transportation and communication systems. However, those people who are elderly and living by themselves have appeared to be at higher risk for health problems. Therefore, it may be speculated that people who have divorced and have not remarried have been at higher risk.

The quality of family ties, more so than just the quantity, may be related to health status in later life. Ward (1979) concluded that the breakup of a marriage affects the quality of family life and kinship ties for men more so than it does for women. Zick and Smith (1991) concluded that a recent transition into being divorced increases the "hazard of mortality" for males. Mergenhagen and colleagues (1985) suggested that although more recently divorced men have reduced (in recent years) their relative risk of death compared with those in other marital statuses, in the 65 years and over category, the divorced have still had the highest mortality rates. It may be proposed that after divorce, later life men are more likely to be at risk for poor physical health and mortality than are women because of at least two factors. First, they are without a spouse to provide the quality of care that later life married men seem to experience. Second, after divorce, men may have fewer contacts and a lower quality of relationship with their children. This may prove to be especially problematic in the latter part of later life, when children could provide care, emotional support, and a variety of services and exchanges (Mancini & Blieszner, 1989).

Based on limited data, Keith (1986a) suggested that among older people, the married have more contact with kin, whereas the unmarried maintain more contact with friends. One study of the divorced and separated (Hyman, 1983) has indicated that 71% of women compared with 38% of men found a great deal of satisfaction with their friendships. Several studies (Lee & Ellithorpe, 1982) have suggested that for life satisfaction and overall well-being in later life, contact with friends seems to be more important than contact with kin. According to Chown (1981), informal social relationships promote psychological well-being in old age, with kinship interactions contributing less to psychological well-being than interaction with friends.

Given the reciprocal influence of psychological well-being and physical health (Menaghan & Lieberman, 1986), informal relationships would appear valuable in promoting and sustaining health (House et al., 1988). Thus, given the pattern of contact with family and friends, divorced later life persons (and especially women) should have equal or better physical health than married. In general, this seems to not be the case. The exact role of social support, caregiving, and kinship ties in maintaining and promoting health needs further specification.

Being divorced would mean one is not living with a spouse and perhaps not living with anyone of the opposite gender. Living alone in middle age and beyond has seemed to present difficulties for men. Mortality rates for men living alone have been 94% higher than those of married men and 40% higher for those who are nonmarried heads of families (Keith, 1986a). Older men living alone may be at greater risk for morbidity, but the cause of this relationship has been unknown. It may be that people have lived alone because they were ill, rather than that living alone somehow led to illness. Among women, however, living alone has not seemed to be a difficult living arrangement. Rather, living in a household with someone else who is head of the household has seemed to be the most destructive for unmarried women (Bernard, 1972; Glenn, 1975, however, have challenged Bernard's idea). Older persons living spouseless (divorced), especially over longer periods of time, may suffer more institutionalization due to a lack of partners to be caregivers when symptoms of illness arise (Fenwick & Barresi, 1981).

The accumulating evidence supports the establishments of a causal relationship between a later life person's social context and his or her health. It also appears that the types and intensity of social relationships vary by marital status. Thus, to understand the relationships among divorce, stress, and health, the social context must be examined.

Context and Health

It appears that resources such as the perception of adequate economic reserves may be related to health among the later life divorced. Social support is another resource that can apparently help buffer the potential ill health effects of stressors. More specifically, perhaps it is an informal network that can provide caregiving and emotional support during times of need (Brubaker, 1990b; Brubaker & Brubaker, 1992b). Divorced later life persons appear to find this resource more among friends than among family. There may also be some relationship, yet relatively unexplored, between one's financial situation and support networks among the divorced in later life. Financial well-being, or its perception, may influence a person's activities in such a way that they enhance the possibilities to establish and/or maintain a viable support network. Without adequate financial resources, a divorced man or woman in later life may be cut off from social contacts due to the inability to afford transportation, entertainment, gifts, or other activities that help to build strong social ties (Hennon, 1983; Mancini & Blieszner, 1989).

Marital status, financial status, and social relationships may interact in another way that influences a later life person's physical health. If divorce is perceived as an indicator that one is a failure, unwanted, or in some other way undesirable or incompetent, this negative appraisal of one's self can potentially affect one's physical health (Coyne & Lazarus, 1980). Appraisals may play an influential role in other ways, for example, how spouses appraise each other's health. Defining one's spouse as ill (or as not ill) can have implications for interactions, health- or help-seeking activities, resource allocations, emotions, and stress. Umberson (1987) directed attention to the social control aspects of marital partners for health behaviors. Without a spouse (or other intimate person) to help validate appraisals of ones health, there may be delays in help-seeking or other primary or preventive health activities. One's financial status could also influence the help-seeking or other activities, such as hospitalization or bed rest (Keith, 1989a). These kinds of actions may be related to one's appraisal of the financial situation (e.g., "Can I afford to take a day off from work?" "Going to the hospital is too expensive."), which then influences the behavioral course of action. Divorce may situate the later life person such that he or she is financially disadvantaged. Divorce may also influence living arrangements and interpersonal contacts that potentially could help validate health appraisals, and also contact with kin or others that may validate appraisals and/or assist in help-seeking or care provision.

One other possibility could be considered. That is, divorced individuals have generally poorer health because they generally have less intimate contacts that validate their sense of worth (see Gove et al., 1990; House et al., 1988, for a review of the association between social relationships/support and health). When one is loved, nurtured, and cared for, validation of the sense of self occurs, and the inherent importance of the person is reinforced. Being valued can be related to being in good emotional health, and good emotional health may be a causal factor in determining the level of physical health. This same line of reasoning might also help explain why not all divorced later life people report poorer health than all married later life people (controlling for selection and other factors affecting health such as maturational-organic factors). If a marriage was conflicted to the point that hostilities or psychopathological factors led to one spouse trying to hurt the other, the cross-validation function of marital (or intimate) communication on appraised health status would have broken down. Likewise, a divorced person may find such intimate communication and functioning with someone other than the spouse. As has been noted, it is the quality of the relationship that is most important in producing positive states of well-being (Gove et al., 1990). There is no reason to assume that all later life intact marriages are happy, well adjusted, and functional (Ade-Ridder & Hennon, 1989; Brubaker, 1985). In fact, they may be quite dysfunctional. On the other hand, it should not be assumed that all divorced later life people are unhappy, distressed, dysfunctional, or isolated.

Stress and Health

The stress of divorce may be displayed in a later life person's health (Gove et al., 1990; Zick & Smith, 1991), not directly due to life changes leading to the depletion of defense mechanisms and thus more opportunistic infections and so forth, but rather more indirectly, through what have been called external loop pathways. These pathways include such things as being at risk due to depletion of financial resources, lack of quality social contacts, and the inability to validate one's self-assessment of current health status or future risk of poor health. In short, the middle-aged or older person's economic and social environments become altered by divorce, which has consequences for the person's emotional and physical well-being. The process of change can be stressful; likewise, the resulting lack of economic and social resources can be stressful.

The evidence would suggest that other interpersonal and intrapersonal factors be investigated to increase contextual understanding of the ways in which divorce, stress, and health in later life are related. Just structural factors like marital status do not tell us much about the pathways and mechanisms influencing health status. Although knowledge of marital status, gender, and socioeconomic status can help alert professionals to possible people at risk, and programs of intervention can perhaps be readied, reliance on marital status as a screening device may in fact hide or conceal many people at risk and focus attention on many people who are not.

To date, it appears that the relationships between marital status and health in later life are complex and not well understood. Individuals' stress management strategies, in a global as well as in a specific sense, should be considered. How later life people appraise divorce and their current situations would appear to be related to both shorter term adjustments and longer term adaptations to this potential stressor (life event) on the somatic, emotional, and social levels. Although intrapersonal factors need to be taken into account, it is also clear that contextual factors appear to place some people in later life more at risk of morbidity and mortality than other people. The resources a person can allocate to counterbalance the demands of divorcing and/or being divorced appear to interact with the appraisal to influence life chances and the quality of life in later life, including one's health.

● ● ●

As a result of a number of changes within our society, individuals' experiences with divorce and the concomitant health situations may differ in the future. For example, enhanced employment opportunities may provide divorced females with a better economic situation and decrease their economic dependency on their former spouses. At the same time, the decreasing pattern of awarding lifetime alimony to former wives relieves men of a long-term economic burden. The increasing pattern of sharing pension and, at times, health benefits provides resources that many past cohorts of divorced women did not have. The stigma of divorce and its possible influence on social support and/or appraisals appear to have been changing. These various changes suggest that divorced middle-aged and older persons' health patterns may differ in the future. More sensitivity for cohort, rather than just aging, explanations of relationships between divorce and health are necessary. There is little doubt that additional research is needed to identify the changing patterns associated with divorce in later life. Consequently, current clinical strategies may need to be altered to effectively work with divorced later life persons in the future.

References

Ade-Ridder, L., & Hennon, C.B. (Eds.). (1989). *Lifestyles of the elderly: Diversity in relationships, health, and caregiving.* New York, NY: Human Sciences Press.

Ahrons, C. (1983). Divorce: Before, during, and after. In H.I. McCubbin & C.R. Figley (Eds.), *Stress and the family: Coping with normative transitions* (pp. 102–115). New York, NY: Brunner/Mazel.

Aldous, J. (1987). New views on the family life of the elderly and the near-elderly. *Journal of Marriage and the Family, 49,* 227–234.

Baum, S.K. (1988). Meaningful life experiences for elderly persons. *Psychological Reports, 63,* 427–433.

Bengtson, V.T. (1986). Sociological perspectives on aging, families and the future. In M. Bergener, M. Ermini, & H.B. Stahelin (Eds.), *Dimensions in aging* (pp. 237–262). London, England: Academic Press.

Bernard, J. (1972). *The future of marriage.* New York, NY: World.

Brody, E.M. (1990). *Women in the middle: Their parentcare years.* New York, NY: Springer.

Brubaker, E., & Brubaker, T.H. (1992a). The context of retired women in caregiving. In M. Szinovacz, D.J. Ekerdt, & B.H. Vinick (Eds.), *Families and retirement* (pp. 222–235). Newbury Park, CA: Sage.

Brubaker, T.H. (1985). *Later life families.* Beverly Hills, CA: Sage.

Brubaker, T.H. (1990a). Families in later life: A burgeoning research area. *Journal of Marriage and the Family, 52,* 959–981.

Brubaker, T.H. (1990b). A contextual approach to the development of stress associated with family caregiving in later life. In M.A.P. Stephens, J.L. Crowther, S.E. Holofitl, & D.L. Tennenbaum (Eds.), *Stress and coping in later life* (pp. 29–47). Washington, DC: Hemisphere.

Brubaker, T.H., & Brubaker, E. (1992b). Family caregiving in the U.S.: An issue of gender differences? In J.I. Kosberg (Ed.), *Family care of the elderly: Social and cultural changes.* Newbury Park, CA: Sage.

Brubaker, T.H., & Hennon, C.B. (1992). Later life divorce and its implications for family life education. *Family Perspective, 26*(1), 11–43.

Bulcroft, K., Bulcroft, R., Hatch, L., & Borgatta, E.F. (1989). Antecedents and consequences of remarriage in later life. *Research on Aging, 11,* 82–106.

Chiriboga, D.A. (1982). Adaptation to marital separation in later and earlier life. *Journal of Gerontology, 37,* 109–114.

Chiriboga, D.A., Roberts, J., & Stein, J. (1978). Psychological well-being during marital separation. *Journal of Divorce, 2,* 21–35.

Chown, S. (1981). Friendship in old age. In S. Duck & R. Gilmore (Eds.), *Personal relationships: 2. Developing personal relationships* (pp. 231–246). New York, NY: Academic Press.

Coyne, J.C., & Lazarus, R. (1980). Cognitive style, stress perception, and coping. In I.L. Kutish, L.B. Schlesinger, & Associates (Eds.), *Handbook on stress and anxiety: Contemporary knowledge, theory, and treatment* (pp. 144–158). San Francisco, CA: Jossey-Bass.

DeShane, M.R., & Brown-Wilson, K. (1981). Divorce in later life: A call for research. *Journal of Divorce, 4,* 81–91.

Farnsworth, J., Pett, M.A., & Lund, D.A. (1989). Predictors of loss management and well-being in later life widowhood and divorce. *Journal of Family Issues, 10,* 102–121.

Fenwick, R., & Barresi, C.M. (1981). Health consequences of marital status change among the elderly: A comparison of cross-sectional and longitudinal analysis. *Journal of Health and Social Behavior, 22,* 106–116.

Fox, J.W. (1980). Gove's specific sex-role theory of mental illness: A research note. *Journal of Health and Social Behavior, 21,* 260–267.

Glenn, N.D. (1975). The contribution of marriage to the psychological well-being of males and females. *Journal of Marriage and the Family, 37,* 594–600.

Glenn, N.D., & Weaver, C.N. (1988). The changing relationship of marital status to reported happiness. *Journal of Marriage and the Family, 50,* 317–324.

Glick, P.C. (1984). Marriage, divorce, and living arrangements. *Journal of Family Issues, 5,* 7–26.

Glick, P.C. (1989). Remarried families, stepfamilies, and stepchildren: A brief demographic profile. *Family Relations, 38,* 24–27.

Gove, W.R. (1972). The relationship between sex roles, marital status, and mental illness. *Social Forces, 51,* 34–45.

Gove, W.R., Style, C.B., & Hughes, M. (1990). The effect of marriage on the well-being of adults: A theoretical analysis. *Journal of Family Issues, 11,* 4–35.

Guarnaccia, P.J., Angel, R., & Worobey, J.L. (1991). The impact of marital status and employment status on depressive affect for Hispanic Americans. *Journal of Community Psychology, 19,* 136–149.

Hagestad, G.O., & Smyer, M. (1982). Dissolving long-term relationships: Patterns of divorcing in middle age. In S. Duck (Ed.), *Personal relationships: 4. Dissolving personal relationships.* New York, NY: Academic Press.

Haring-Hidore, M., Stock, W.A., Okun, M.A., & Witter, R.A. (1985). Marital status and subjective well-being: A research synthesis. *Journal of Marriage and the Family, 47,* 947–953.

Hennon, C.B. (1983). Divorce and the elderly: A neglected area of research. In T.H. Brubaker (Ed.), *Family relationships in later life* (pp. 149–172). Beverly Hills, CA: Sage.

Hennon, C.B., Brubaker, E., & Kaplan, L. (1991). Health, housing, and aging: Families as case managers. *Journal of Home Economics, 83*(1), 54–62.

Hess, B.B., & Waring, J. (1983). Family relationships of older women: A women's issue. In E.W. Markson (Ed.), *Older women: Issues and prospects* (pp. 227–251). Lexington, MA: D.C. Health.

Himmelfarb, S. (1984). Age and sex differences in the mental health of older persons. *Journal of Consulting and Clinical Psychology, 52*, 844–856.

Holmes, T.H., & Rahe, R.H. (1967). The social readjustment rating scale. *Journal of Psychosomatic Research, 11*, 213–218.

House, J.S., Landis, K.R., & Umberson, D. (1988). Social relationships and health. *Science, 241*, 540–545.

House, J.S., & Robbins, C. (1983). Age, psychosocial stress, and health. In M.W. Riley, B.B. Hess, & K. Bond (Eds.), *Aging in society: Selected reviews of recent research* (pp. 175–197). Hillsdale, NJ: Lawrence Erlbaum.

Hyman, H. (1983). *Of time and widowhood.* Durham, NC: Duke University Press.

Katschke-Jennings, B., & Healy, D. (1987). Remarriage and the elderly. *Journal of Religion and Aging, 3*, 1–11.

Keith, P.M. (1985). Financial well-being of older divorced/separated men and women: Findings from a panel study. *Journal of Divorce, 9*, 61–72.

Keith, P.M. (1986a). Isolation of the unmarried in later life. *Family Relations, 35*, 389–395.

Keith, P.M. (1986b). The social context and resources of the unmarried in old age. *International Journal of Aging and Human Development, 23*, 81–96.

Keith, P.M. (1989a). Postponement of health care by widowed, divorced, and never-married older men. In L. Ade-Ridder & C.B. Hennon (Eds.), *Lifestyles of the elderly: Diversity in relationships, health, and caregiving* (pp. 173–184). New York, NY: Human Sciences Press.

Keith, P.M. (1989b). *The unmarried in later life.* New York, NY: Praeger.

Keith, P.M., & Lorenz, F.O. (1989). Financial strain and health of unmarried older people. *The Gerontologist, 29*, 684–691.

Kessler, R.C., & Essex, M. (1982). Marital status and depression: The importance of coping resources. *Social Forces, 61*, 484–507.

Kessler, R.C., & McRae, J.A., Jr. (1984). A note on the relationships of sex and marital status to psychological distress. *Research in Community and Mental Health, 4*, 109–130.

Kincaid, S.B., & Caldwell, R.A. (1991). Initiator status, family support, and adjustment to marital separation: A test of an interaction hypothesis. *Journal of Community Psychology, 19*, 79–88.

Lee, G.R., & Ellithorpe, E. (1982). Intergenerational exchange and subjective well-being among the elderly. *Journal of Marriage and the Family, 44*, 217–224.

Lee, G.R., Seccombe, K., & Shehan, C.L. (1991). Marital status and personal happiness: An analysis of trend data. *Journal of Marriage and the Family, 53*, 839–844.

Mancini, J.A., & Blieszner, R. (1989). Aging parents and adult children: Research themes in intergenerational relationships. *Journal of Marriage and the Family, 51*, 275–290.

Martin, T.C., & Bumpass, L.L. (1989). Recent trends in marital disruption. *Demography, 26*, 37–51.

McCubbin, H.I., & Patterson, J.M. (1983). Family transitions: Adaptation to stress. In H.I. McCubbin & C.R. Figley (Eds.), *Stress and the family: Coping with normative transitions* (pp. 5–25). New York, NY: Brunner/ Mazel.

McCullough, J., & Zick, C.D. (1992). The roles of role strain, economic resources and time demands in explaining mothers' life satisfaction. *Journal of Family and Economic Issues, 13,* 23–44.

McKinley, J.B., McKinley, S.M., & Brambilla, D. (1987). The relative contribution of endocrine changes and social circumstances to depression in mid-aged women. *Journal of Health and Social Behavior, 28,* 345–363.

Mechanic, D. (1974). Discussion of research programs on relations between stressful life events and episodes of physical illness. In B.S. Dohrenwend & B.P. Dohrenwend (Eds.), *Stressful life events: Their nature and effects* (pp. 89–97). New York, NY: Wiley.

Menaghan, E.G., & Lieberman, M.A. (1986). Changes in depression following divorce: A panel study. *Journal of Marriage and the Family, 48,* 319–328.

Mergenhagen, P.M., Lee, B.A., & Gove, W.R. (1985). Till death do us part: Recent changes in the relationship between marital stress and mortality. *Sociology and Social Research, 70,* 53–56.

Mikhail, A. (1981). Stress: A psychophysiological conception. *Journal of Human Stress, 7,* 9–15.

Moen, P., & Howery, C.B. (1988). The significance of time in the study of families under stress. In D.M. Klein & J. Aldous (Eds.), *Social stress and family development* (pp. 131–156). New York, NY: Guilford.

Morgan, L.A. (1991). *After marriage ends: Economic consequences for midlife women.* Newbury Park, CA: Sage.

National Center for Health Statistics. (1991). Advance report of final divorce statistics, 1988. *Monthly Vital Statistics Report, 39*(12), Suppl. 2 (DHHS Publication No. (PHS) 91-1120). Hyattsville, MD: Public Health Service.

Newberry, B.H., Baldwin, D.R., Madden, J.E., & Gerstenberger, T.J. (1987). Stress and disease: An assessment. In J.H. Humphrey (Ed.), *Human stress: Current selected research* (pp. 123–151). New York, NY: AMS Press.

Norton, A.J., & Moorman, J.E. (1987). Current trends in marriage and divorce among American women. *Journal of Marriage and the Family, 49,* 3–14.

Pett, M.A., & Vaughan-Cole, B. (1986). The impact of income issues and social status on post-divorce adjustment of custodial parents. *Family Relations, 35,* 103–111.

Preston, M. (1984). Children and the elderly: Divergent paths for America's dependents. *Demography, 21,* 435–457.

Renne, K.S. (1971). Health and marital experience in an urban population. *Journal of Marriage and the Family, 33,* 338–350.

Rose, R.M., & Levin, M.A. (1979). The crisis in stress research: A critical reappraisal of the role of stress in hypertension, gastrointestinal illness, and female reproductive dysfunction [Special Issue]. *Journal of Human Stress, 5*(2).

Ross, C.E. (1991). Marriage and the sense of control. *Journal of Marriage and the Family, 53*, 831–838.

Schoen, R., Urton, W., Woodrow, K., & Baj, J. (1985). Marriage and divorce in twentieth century Americans cohorts. *Demography, 22*, 101–114.

Selye, H. (1980). The stress concept today. In I.L. Kutish, L.B. Schlesinger, & Associates (Eds.), *Handbook on stress and anxiety: Contemporary knowledge, theory, and treatment* (pp. 127–143). San Francisco, CA: Jossey-Bass.

Thoits, P.A. (1986). Multiple identities: Examining gender and marital status differences in distress. *American Sociological Review, 51*, 259–272.

Uhlenberg, P., & Myers, M.P. (1981). Divorce and the elderly. *The Gerontologist, 21*, 276–282.

Umberson, D. (1987). Family status and health behaviors: Social control as a dimension of social integration. *Journal of Health and Social Behavior, 28*, 306–319.

Verbrugge, L.M. (1979). Marital status and health. *Journal of Marriage and the Family, 41*, 267–285.

Verbrugge, L.M. (1983). Multiple roles and physical health of women and men. *Journal of Health and Social Behavior, 24*, 16–30.

Voydanoff, P. (1990). Economic distress and family relations: A review of the eighties. *Journal of Marriage and the Family, 52*, 1099–1115.

Ward, R. (1979). The never-married in later life. *Journal of Gerontology, 34*, 861–869.

Weitzman, L.J. (1985). *The divorce revolution: The unexpected social and economic consequences for women and children in America.* New York, NY: Free Press.

Williams, D.G. (1988). Gender, marriage, and psychological well-being. *Journal of Family Issues, 9*, 452–468.

Zick, C.D., & Smith, K.R. (1991). Marital transitions, poverty, and gender differences in mortality. *Journal of Marriage and the Family, 53*, 327–336.

■ ■ ■

PART II

COMMON THERAPEUTIC TECHNIQUES

4

Painful Partings: Providing Therapeutic Guidance

Florence W. Kaslow, PhD

It was Monday morning, and the phone rang at the office. Through tears, the unknown female caller blurted out,

> Please, I *must* have an appointment today. My life is falling apart, and I have no one else to turn to. I came home last night from a weekend visit to my daughter's and found my husband had moved out. His note said he had reached the point of no return. I don't believe it! I'm confused, hurt, desperate. (A choking sob and pause)

This all-too-familiar story evoked empathy and sadness for Claudia's unanticipated loss and her bewildered state. Because the calendar for the day was full, but it seemed insensitive to make her wait another day wallowing in her anguish, an appointment was offered for what would normally be after hours.

Claudia arrived early. The secretary noted that she could barely sit still to fill out the short intake forms. A friend accompanied her because she was too agitated to drive. Her story, as it unfolded during the first session, was of course unique in the details while also being similar to the general facts.

> Claudia and Phil had been married for 24 years. She was 46 years old, and he was 49. She had been planning a joint celebration for their 25th anniversary and his 50th birthday, unaware that he was planning to exit from the marriage. She kept reiterating that she was totally unaware that such a cataclysm was about to befall her.

In appearance, underneath the swollen eyes and pale face, Claudia was attractive. She was well groomed and obviously kept her figure in shape. She swam, bicycled, played tennis, and did aerobics. She reported that Phil was also into physical exercise; some activities they did together, and Phil also participated in triathalon events. She was articulate and bright and in a state of almost shock. Her thoughts tumbled forth in rapid, staccato sentences.

Their son, Jerry (age 21), had just entered his last year of college and was living at his on-campus fraternity house. He was a good student and was planning to go to law school the following year. Their daughter, Felice (age 23), had gotten an MBA and was working on Wall Street. She had recently married, and Claudia had flown to New York, at the newlyweds' request, to help them in settling into their new apartment. When her husband had said goodbye at the airport 5 days before, he had kissed her lightly and told her to have a great time and sent his love to the kids. Nothing had seemed amiss.

After telling her that I recognized her agony and distress and that I would do all I could to help her cope with her dismay, I queried if, in retrospect, there were any signs of his being restless or discontented and whether there had been any noticeable changes in his behavior.

Claudia became pensive and quiet. She recalled that Phil had told her several times in the past year that life had become routine and dull, and he missed the old sense of excitement and dreams. He voiced envy over their daughter's enthusiasm for her future and had said he wished he were young and full of optimism again. He had told her he dreaded turning 50. She had made light of it—saying the alternative was worse—and had become immersed in engagement, wedding, and shower plans. She also recollected that he had been working more evenings than usual. She had attributed this to their need for additional income to defray the wedding expenses and continuing high costs of their son's college and projected graduate school. There had been a decrease in their sexual play, and although she had missed the intimacy, she had felt sure things would get back to normal after the wedding was over, all the house guests had gone, and their son returned to college at the end of his summer vacation at home.

Claudia was seen three more times in the next 10 days. She was frantic until Thursday (3 days after the first session) because she had no word from Phil and no idea of his whereabouts. She had called his office and had been told he was away for the week on a business trip. His secretary was surprised that his wife didn't know this. He was traveling and they did not know where he actually was.

A proud person, Claudia felt thoroughly humiliated. She didn't want to press the secretary for more information and make her private affair an item of gossip in her husband's office. Obviously, the trip and the "deception" had been planned. Her astonishment and hurt grew. By Thursday she was disconsolate and asked, "How could I have been such a fool? I was happily married, loved him dearly, and always thought it was reciprocated. I never would have thought him capable of such treachery."

When Phil finally called Thursday night, he said he was sorry she had been so worried, but it was the only way he could leave. He had made up his mind that he wanted a divorce; the decision was irrevocable. He had wanted to avoid all scenes, and this was the only way he could do it. Claudia reported she had tried to reason with him and say it was a passing phase and he'd settle down, and that if he told her what was wrong she'd do her best to change it and was sure they could recapture their love and friendship. He said this was not possible. She implored him not to destroy the family and to come with her for marital therapy. He adamantly refused, saying nothing she could do would change his mind. Finally he confessed, "I found someone else. She's young and beautiful and with her I feel young again—alive and sensuous. She thinks I'm 45 and look like 40 and that's the way I want it."

He indicated that the business trip was a pleasure trip and that his "love" was with him. Claudia was dumbfounded and outraged and screamed, "How could you do this to us?" He retorted that he needed to get out, that he was no longer willing to be "the perfect husband and father"; now he was going to "put himself first" and that was that, and he hung up.

Underlying Themes

In this case illustration, we find many of the dynamics and themes that repetitively appear when divorce occurs. These themes are elaborated next.

Yearning for Youthfulness

At a time of major transition in the individual and family life cycle (Carter & McGoldrick, 1980; Erikson, 1968), there are tasks to be undertaken and completed and decisions to be made. Phil was not ready to accept that he had a child old enough to be married, that he was at the point of having a silver wedding anniversary, and that he was about to turn 50 years of age. He decided to deny this reality by discarding the wife who symbolized it and replacing her with a much younger and more frivolous playmate. His yearning for youthfulness soon was also expressed in his purchasing a red sports car to replace his sedate grey BMW.

Poor Communication and Gradual Estrangement

Phil and Claudia had gradually ceased communicating well with one another. He had withdrawn from frequent verbal and sexual expressiveness and turned outward for satisfaction of his emotional needs. She had negated his requests for more attention and excitement and had been, to his thinking, overly preoccupied with their home, their daughter's wedding festivities, and their church and community. He wanted to put himself first "before it was too late"; she thought she had always put him first and that basically her world had revolved around his needs. The estrangement was subtle, gradual, and, from one partner's view, irreparable. It is easier to understand when a partner leaves after years of "putting up with" alcoholism, drug abuse, physical abuse, neglect or total indifference, humiliation, and disrespect in public. It is initially incomprehensible to be rejected for being "too good" and "doing all the right things," as Claudia had. Apparently, Phil believed he had also done all the right things as a husband and father, provider, and pillar of the community. He had become totally bored with the repetitiveness of his proper life-style. He wanted fun, excitement, and even some "naughtiness" to spice up his life before it was too late.

Disruption of All Family Members' Lives

Claudia entered therapy at the beginning of Station I of the separation process—*the emotional divorce* (see the Appendix entitled "Diaclectic Model of Stages in the Divorce Process"; Bohannan, 1970; Kaslow, 1979/1980, 1981, 1990). She was overwhelmed by grief, disbelief, anguish, and bewilderment. Because she had no prior conscious awareness of her husband's contemplated departure, she was sorely traumatized. Initially, an attempt was made to establish therapeutic rapport by joining with her through listening to her confused outpourings and accepting how miserable she felt. During the next few sessions, her hurt and anger erupted and were validated. We used batacas in the session so she could physically vent some of her rage. She was urged to resume her aerobics classes and her tennis to release some of the tension. We explored what was so frightening—shifting back and forth between rejection, loneliness, and the disruption of her total life. Because she had sufficient funds to carry her during the first month, and Phil had called to say, "Don't worry—I will be generous and fair in the financial settlement" and had sent whatever money she was requesting temporarily, we did not begin to focus on the legal (Station II) and economic (Station III) aspects of divorce (Kaslow, 1987; Kaslow & Schwartz, 1987) until approximately 6 weeks after treatment commenced.

It seemed more important to first bolster up her severely bruised self-image through ego-supportive therapy and to help her regain some modicum of control over her own life. For quite a while, she felt Phil had thrown her into uncharted, deep water and left her there to sink. Therapy was therefore conceptualized as her life raft, and at each session she took more responsibility for determining its course. As is typical, progress was slow and uneven. Sometimes she saw the sea as very stormy and likened the huge waves of feelings she encountered to the roller coaster phenomena I had used to describe the early phase of the divorce process.

Distress of Adult Children

Claudia had told the children about their father's departure right after she found he had moved out. They, too, were nonplussed and infuriated. They had perceived their parents as loving and in love, their home as stable and predictable. They had great devotion to and admiration for their father. Neither had any idea that he had another personal life outside of the family. Like their mother, they felt betrayed (Wallerstein & Kelly, 1980). Dad had always stressed the importance of loyalty (Boszormenyi-Nagy & Spark, 1973, 1984) and honesty, and they had incorporated these ideals as core values in their individual and family code of beliefs and behavior. Thus, mother and young adult children spoke daily by phone commiserating with one another. This support was vital to Claudia, who saw herself and the children as innocent victims of Phil's duplicity and the "other woman's" conniving.

The fact that Phil did not call or write to his children for 3 weeks added to their confusion, distrust, and anger. When he did and relayed how ecstatic he was and asked them to be happy for him, they told him and later Claudia that they were incredulous. There was no apology for disrupting their lives or for the crushing of the family unit. He was completely engulfed in his own hedonistic pleasure and seemed baffled by their cool responses. He chastised them for siding with their mother and pondered aloud what terrible things she must have said about him. Separately both retorted along the lines that his behavior spoke for itself; Mom did not have to elaborate. When they were not delighted to hear from him and arrange to meet his lover as soon as possible, he said, "If that is the appreciation I get for all the years of my life that I was your generous and doting dad, you just might find yourselves disinherited." Both Felice and Jerry were astounded; the father they knew and loved was neither selfish nor punitive. They could not fathom what had occurred.

In this instance, Claudia's adult children resided out of town and constituted a daily support system for their mother (Station V— community divorce; Bohannan, 1970; Kaslow, 1990—also extended family divorce). It was agreed that they did not need to experience further severe perturbations in their lives. Jerry had to remain in school and try to concentrate and keep his grades high enough to be doing well when he applied for graduate school. Felice was attempting to juggle her new job and new husband while seeking to comfort Mom and assuage her distress over the chain of events. The daily three-way contact they maintained seemed the best course of action. Claudia did not want to place additional demands on them and knew "they are there for me."

Disillusionment and Shattered Dreams

Initially, the rejected spouse has the most difficult time. He or she feels spurned, cast off, and unwanted, and, indeed, this is true. In addition to feeling hurt and angry, and sometimes desirous of retaliating, spouses who have been rejected suffer a loss of self-esteem and confidence (Kaslow & Schwartz, 1987). The sense of bewilderment is pervasive because the dreams and plans for the present and future have been dismantled and will probably take a minimum of 2 to 4 years to be replaced. Divorce therapy entails helping them pick up the pieces, minus the spouse, and rearranging them in a new mosaic that ultimately may be appealing and satisfying but that is quite different from the one pursued earlier.

Later, the spouse who sought the separation, and who may have felt relief and jubilance about leaving a relationship that had become stale, irritating, or intolerable for him or her, may find a buildup of remorse, guilt, and/or a sense of loss. As time elapses, he or she may miss the family as a unit, holiday and special event celebrations, the history that they had built and shared, and the memories of the good times. As they see the hurt inflicted that was not intended, some wonder, "Was it worth it?" (Others like the new life they create and wonder why they did not extricate from a deleterious relationship earlier.) However, it was much too early in the divorce of Phil and Claudia for any of this to have surfaced in Phil's heart and mind.

One of the dilemmas of a systems therapist who does divorce work is to maintain a systems perspective. This undergirds all of my work even when, as in the case described herein, I am only seeing one member of the family system because the others are unwilling or unable to attend, and/or it seems counterindicated.

Conflicting Needs of the Former Partners—Case Dynamics and Interventions

When Phil called again several weeks after his "disappearance" to give Claudia his new address and phone number in case of an emergency and to tell her he was filing for divorce as soon as his attorney could draw up the papers, so she could expect to be served soon (Station III—legal), she tried to slow things down. She pleaded with him to have dinner with her and explain more to her as she had a desperate need to understand what had gone awry. He refused, saying he had no desire to rehash the past. Next, she asked if he would come to just one therapy session to help her make sense of it all. Again he refused, saying, "I feel terrific and have no problems now. You have the problems and will have to solve them without my help." His detachment and his complete negation of her emotional needs was incomprehensible to her. She could not fathom how someone could suddenly act as if there had never been a deep bond and could disregard the former loved one's request for some clarification and information.

I was able to reinterpret this as perhaps "a blessing in disguise" because her heightened disappointment and anger made it impossible for her to continue to cling to a fantasy of eventual reunion. The anger gave momentum to her dawning realization of his current insensitivity and to the many insensitivities and negations she had overlooked in the past. It contributed toward her willingness to begin to let go of her idealized vision of Phil.

In the author's opinion, when cases evolve in this type of sequence, individual therapy constitutes the treatment of choice within an interactive systems perspective. Claudia needed all of the therapist's attention for herself; she had to feel worthy of all of the time and energy being devoted to her story and her needs. The first task was to enable Claudia to stay functional and not become so depressed that she hid under the covers, something she felt like doing many mornings. Once this was accomplished and she regained some sense of self, she was encouraged to see friends who felt safe to her (Station V—community/friends/family) and to begin looking at her current economic picture and future financial needs (Station III—economic). The impact of her decisions and behaviors on her future and that of her children was considered throughout.

Because there were no minor children and the settlement Phil offered was equitable and fair, and because Florida divorce law sanctions no-fault divorce and equitable distributions of property, Claudia accepted his terms with relatively few modifications. Despite her aching heart, she recognized that she did not want a husband who no longer wanted her and that there was nothing to be gained by contesting his petition for divorce.

The whole legal process progressed much more rapidly than occurs when there are custody issues to resolve. The final hearing took place and the decree was issued within 6 months of Phil's departure, long before Claudia had reached psychic resolution (Station VII; Kaslow, 1988).

Guilt and Innocence

Before this could occur, we worked on Claudia's view that she was the innocent victim and he was the guilty perpetrator of the divorce. It took well over a year before she had healed enough to be able to tolerate exploring what she may have contributed to the demise of the marriage.

> Gradually she recognized that she was so intent on being the good wife and mother and doing everything right that she had become serious and perfectionistic. She had not been or had much fun. Also, the wife/mother/volunteer *par excellence* roles had eclipsed the lover and playful friend roles.
>
> She remembered that occasionally Phil had said he wished they could have more fun and get away for adventuresome vacations and that she had disregarded his comments. Further, she realized that she had "been replaced" by someone who resonated to Phil's request for "fun and games." She wondered why he hadn't been more insistent and still felt the burden of responsibility for the actual decision to divorce was his—that he should have either forced the issue with her and/or told her more directly that the marriage was floundering and he thought they should go for professional help. She continued to see him as "more culpable" on all levels, but did increasingly take cognizance of her contribution to her husband's disappointment in their spousal relationship.

Is There Life Beyond Divorce?

At this juncture, Claudia began to try to loosen up and joined a "Single Again" adult group. When we phased out and then terminated therapy after 15 months, her self-esteem had been restored, she was working part time as an interior designer using her art and decorating background, and she was still active in sports and other physical activities. She was more relaxed, her daily contacts with the children had diminished, and they were able to have occasional visits with their father, although they still refused to meet his "mistress"—the other woman. She was beginning to date despite the paucity of available healthy men in the 50- to 60-year-old age bracket who were willing to date a woman over 40. She ultimately wanted to remarry and felt she could risk trusting again. She now savored some time alone after long periods of fearing and disliking the loneliness that permeated the immediate postdivorce period. She was uncertain that she would meet someone with whom she could feel happy, comfortable, and secure, and with whom she would again be a sensuous woman. Parts of many sessions were devoted to how and where she could meet eligible men and what constituted safe and sane psychosocial behavior in the early 1990s. This was also a topic of discussion periodically at her "Singles Again" group, which had provided a good place to make new friends and to exchange views on divorce and feelings about dating, sex, and remarriage.

Because Claudia and Phil had been married in church, she wanted to be divorced in the eyes of the church as well as under the aegis of the civil court. She approached her minister about performing a religious divorce ceremony (Station IV—religion; Kaslow, 1990). He was not comfortable with the idea and said the church had no such ritual. I told Claudia about a therapeutic divorce ceremony I sometimes do, and this is in the offing for the next time her children are home for the holidays. She will ask Phil to join her and if he refuses, she will ask one of her divorced male friends to participate in his stead (Kaslow, 1992; Kaslow & Schwartz, 1987). She believes this will help her to achieve greater closure on her marriage to Phil and move into the next chapters in her life (Station VII—the psychic divorce).

Summary and Conclusions

Divorce at any stage of the life cycle is a complex and agonizing process. The discontent, disappointment, and disenchantment that are experienced prior to the decision to separate frequently crystallize when other major transitions in the family are occurring and precipitate a reevaluation of the state of the marital union. In middle-aged couples, once the children have left home permanently, they are alone with one another. Many of the deficits one or both experience in the marriage surface and no longer are denied or put on hold, now that the children are grown. This is particularly true if one partner feels he or she has served his or her time and now is free to depart, as the children have done. Often if he or she has been harboring a desire to separate for a long time, he or she has already done some of the grief work about the demise of the marriage and may be, or appear to be, quite insensitive to the shock and bereavement of the rejected partner.

Frequently, the desire to dissolve the marriage is propelled by a wish for more fun, freedom, novelty, adventure, and new experience. After 25-plus years of wedlock, the mate tends to be too predictable, too familiar, and often is perceived as dull. Spouses know each other's every thought and mood, and there are no ideas, interests, or new pathways to explore together. The grown childrens' ambitions, accomplishments, and exciting voyages into new terrain stir up repressed longings to see a wider world and partake in what it has to offer. The challenges of life beyond divorce beckon more strongly to those who decide to separate than the safe, secure realm of life with the long-time spouse.

For others, "getting out" is a matter of survival. They realize they have already stayed too long in marriages where a partner has been physically violent and/or verbally abusive. They have seen their spouse inebriated or stoned once too often. They can no longer tolerate feeling unworthy, unloved, neglected, or imprisoned. They decide to extricate, knowing that even loneliness is preferable to continued turbulence and overt or covert conflict. Often the abusive or addicted spouse is shocked at the unexpected defection; he or she never anticipated that the codependent mate would really leave and not return.

Other factors that contribute to mid-life divorce include the realization of one's own mortality. Friends become ill and die. One's energy level begins to wane, and it becomes more difficult to stay in shape physically. The desire to live fully, before it is too late, may become pervasive in one's thinking. If he or she meets an attractive potential lover who seems to herald promise of a fuller, more gratifying future, divorce may loom as a necessary stairway to the next horizon. If the affair predates the separation and provides a sense of revitalization and ego satisfaction, the divorce may be pursued avidly.

Initially, the partner who feels rejected has the more difficult time acclimating to a new and unwanted reality. He or she often experiences anger, bitterness, self-recrimination, and a desire to retaliate for the hurt. Disbelief is mingled with acrimony. Fears of loneliness, financial disaster, coping with the totality of life alone, physical illness, and rejection by other family members and friends add to the sense of emotional despondency. Generally, women over 45 years of age have a much more difficult time meeting eligible members of the opposite gender than their male counterparts do, if and when they want to date and to consider remarriage. Questions about one's overall appeal, attractiveness, and sexuality come to the fore. Confidence ebbs for a period of time.

•   •   •

Therapy has to assist the client in attending to what has to be done, like changing titles of ownership on cars and securities, relocating one's residence, changing career, and renegotiating one's relationship with parents, children, and/or grandchildren, as well as the feelings to be resolved. It needs to be flexible and follow the flow and rhythm of the patient's needs for understanding, acceptance, encouragement, and formulation of new dreams and goals and a realistic plan for how to achieve them. The clinician should be able to impart optimism (Beavers & Kaslow, 1981) about the future as he or she guides the patient toward psychic reintegration and a strong sense of self. Becoming whole and healthy, and eager to avail oneself of the opportunities life can afford may take 2 to 4 years from the initial separation. Reassuring patients (and sometimes their significant others) that the journey may be long and arduous, and that a slow recuperation phase is normal, helps assuage some of the agony and facilitates progressive rather than regressive thoughts and actions. Beyond the painful parting, there is life after divorce in the middle years, and it can be endowed with meaning and satisfaction.

References

Beavers, W.R., & Kaslow, F.W. (1981). The anatomy of hope. *Journal of Marital and Family Therapy, 7*(2), 119–126.

Bohannan, P. (1970). The six stations of divorce. In P. Bohannon (Ed.), *Divorce and after: An analysis of the emotional and social problems of divorce* (pp. 27–55). New York, NY: Doubleday.

Boszormenyi-Nagy, I., & Spark, G. (1973). *Invisible loyalties.* New York, NY: Harper & Row. [Reprinted 1984. New York, NY: Brunner/Mazel.]

Carter, E., & McGoldrick, M. (Eds.). (1980). *The family life cycle.* New York, NY: Gardner Press.

Erikson, E.H. (1968). *Identity: Youth and crisis.* New York, NY: Norton.

Kaslow, F.W. (1979/1980). Stages in the divorce process: A psycholegal perspective. *Villanova Law Review, 25*(4/5), 718–751.

Kaslow, F.W. (1981). Divorce and divorce therapy. In A. Gurman & D. Kniskern (Eds.), *Handbook of family therapy* (pp. 662–696). New York, NY: Brunner/Mazel.

Kaslow, F.W. (1984). Divorce: An evolutionary process of change in the family system. *Journal of Divorce, 7*(3), 21–39.

Kaslow, F.W. (1987). Stages in the divorce process: Dynamics and treatment. In F.W. Kaslow & L.L. Schwartz (Eds.), *The dynamics of divorce: A life cycle perspective* (pp. 23–37). New York, NY: Brunner/Mazel.

Kaslow, F.W. (1988). The psychological dimension of divorce mediation. In J. Folberg & A. Milne (Eds.), *Divorce mediation: Theory and practice* (pp. 83–108). New York, NY: Guilford.

Kaslow, F.W. (1990). Divorce therapy and mediation for better custody. *Japanese Journal of Family Psychology, 4,* 1937. [In English]

Kaslow, F.W. (1992). The divorce ceremony: A healing strategy. In T. Nelson & T. Trepper (Eds.), *101 favorite family therapy interventions.* New York, NY: Haworth Press.

Kaslow, F.W., & Schwartz, L.L. (1987). *Dynamics of divorce: A life cycle perspective.* New York, NY: Brunner/Mazel.
Wallerstein, J.S., & Kelly, J.B. (1980). *Surviving the breakup: How children and parents cope with divorce.* New York, NY: Basic Books.

■ ■ ■

Appendix
Diaclectic Model of Stages in the Divorce Process

Divorce Stage	Station	Stage	Feelings	Actions and Tasks	Therapeutic Interventions	Mediation
Predivorce A time of deliberation and despair	I. Emotional divorce	A	Disillusionment Dissatisfaction Alienation Anxiety Disbelief	Avoiding the issue Sulking and/or crying Confronting partner Quarreling	Marital therapy (one couple) Couples group therapy	
		B	Despair Dread Anguish Ambivalence Shock Emptiness Anger Chaos Inadequacy Low self-esteem Loss Depression Detachment Anger	Experiencing denial Experiencing withdrawal (physical and emotional) Pretending all is fine Attempting to win back affection Asking friends, family, clergy for advice	Marital therapy (one couple) Divorce therapy Couples group therapy	

Divorce Stage	Station	Stage	Feelings	Actions and Tasks	Therapeutic Interventions	Mediation
During divorce A time of legal involvement	II. Legal divorce	C	Self-pity Helplessness	Bargaining Screaming Threatening Attempting suicide Consulting an attorney or mediator	Family therapy Individual adult therapy Child therapy	Set the stage for mediation-oriented session. Ascertain parties' understanding of the process and its appropriateness for them.
	III. Economic divorce	D	Confusion Fury Sadness Loneliness Relief Vindictiveness	Separating physically Filing for legal divorce Considering financial settlement Deciding on custody/visitation schedule	Children of divorce group therapy Child therapy Adult therapy	Define the rules of mediation. Identify the issues, and separate therapeutic issues from mediation issues. Focus on parental strengths, children's needs, and formulation of best possible co-parenting and residential arrangement.

Stage		Feelings	Tasks	Therapeutic Intervention	
IV. Co-parental divorce and the problems of custody	E	Concern for children Ambivalence Numbness Uncertainty	Grieving and mourning Telling relatives and friends Reentering work world (unemployed woman) Feeling empowered to make choices	Same as above plus family therapy	Negotiate and process the issues and choices. Reach agreement. Analyze and formalize agreement.
V. Community divorce	F	Indecisiveness Optimism Resignation Excitement Curiosity Regret Sadness	Finalizing divorce Reaching out to new friends Undertaking new activities Stabilizing new lifestyle and daily routine for children Exploring new interests and possibly taking new job	Adults Individual therapy Children Play therapy Group therapy	
VI. Religious divorce	G	Self-doubt Desire for church approval Fear of God's displeasure or wrath	Gaining church acceptance Having a religious divorce ceremony administered Making peace with spiritual self	Divorce ceremony for total family Adult therapy Pastoral counseling	

Divorce Stage	Station	Stage	Feelings	Actions and Tasks	Therapeutic Interventions	Mediation
Postdivorce A time of exploration and reequilibration	VII. Psychic divorce	H	Acceptance Self-confidence Energy Self-worth Wholeness Exhilaration Independence Autonomy	Resynthesizing identity Completing psychic divorce Seeking new love object and making a commitment to some permanency Becoming comfortable with new lifestyle and friends Helping children accept finality of parents' divorce and their continuing relationship with both parents	Parent–child therapy Family therapy Group therapies Children's activity group therapy	Return to mediation when changed circumstances require a negotiation of the agreement.

Sources: Kaslow, F.W. (1984). Divorce: An evolutionary process of change in the family system. *Journal of Divorce, 7*(3), 21–39. Kaslow, F.W. (1988). The psychological dimension of divorce mediation. In J. Folberg & A. Milne (Eds.), *Divorce mediation: Theory and practice.* New York, NY: Guilford.

Note: This is a revised and expanded version. All stations except religion are taken from the work of Bohannan (1973). This addition is original. The process of mediation was not an element of the initial diaclectic model (Kaslow, 1984). It has been added subsequently to illustrate the interface between the process of divorce and mediation.

5

Interesting Cases from a Therapist's Notebook: Interview with Sidney D. Segal

Lita Linzer Schwartz, PhD

The authors of the other chapters in this volume have each taken a stance regarding mid-life divorce issues appropriate to their experiences. In this case, a therapist was interviewed and asked to describe some of his less typical cases involving couples in mid-life and offer his thoughts on divorce prevention. The therapist is Sidney D. Segal, EdD, who is licensed for private practice as a psychologist in Pennsylvania and Arizona, and who practices in southeastern Pennsylvania. In addition, he is a lecturer at Pennsylvania State University, Ogontz Campus, Abington, Pennsylvania.

LLS: Sid, we're all familiar with couples who come for help either because they have lost the ability to communicate with each other, because of mid-life crises, or because one spouse has fallen in love with a third party. Apparently you've had some clients, however, who take these common themes to the extreme. Could you share the gist of some of these cases?

SDS: As it happens, just in the past 2 years there are a few cases that stand out. Three of the couples are separated, en route to divorce, and I've seen them at different points along the way because at least one of the partners wanted to resolve the differences in a positive way if possible. Each of these couples has carried the marital war well beyond what most of us would consider typical of marital conflict.

In the case of Sam and Carol, for example, we have a fairly late marriage. Sam is 47, a very gentle man, and Carol is a few years younger. They have been married for 13 years and have three children. Last year, Carol decided, and said, that she had "outgrown" Sam and that she had a "friend." The friend apparently visited several times when Sam was not at home, and Carol made no attempt to hide this, even to the point of leaving his cigarette butts in the ashtray for Sam to see. This continued for a few months, much to Sam's growing consternation. Finally, Sam brought some acid home from his business. As it turned out, the next morning the "friend" came to take Carol to work. Sam "flipped out," and threw acid in the friend's face, fortunately causing only minor injury.

Needless to say, Sam was arrested, tried, convicted, and sentenced, although the judge was sympathetic to the underlying cause of Sam's action and gave him a minimum sentence of 60 days. Interestingly enough, Carol's mother had been a character witness for her son-in-law at the trial, which gives further indication of his more normal personality. Sam lost his job as a data processor as a result of his conviction and sentence and has been unable to find another. There *is* that question on employment forms about ever having been in prison, which, if answered honestly, usually causes personnel officers not to hire a person, and if answered dishonestly, leads to firing when the lie is discovered. His wife knows that he is unemployed, but is dunning him for support. Meanwhile, she has moved into her friend's house; the friend will not allow Sam to park in his driveway to pick up the children on visitation days, and his record puts him at risk for visitation altogether.

Sam still hoped to salvage the marriage when he was released, partly because he still loved his wife and also was concerned about the three children. He's been in therapy for several months and is beginning to recognize the taunting nature of his wife's behavior before the acid-throwing incident. In fact, he's becoming convinced that she may have orchestrated the full sequence of events so that she could get out of the marriage, keep the children, *and* ruin him in the process.

To balance the picture in terms of gender, there is also the local politician, who we'll call Jim, who had a very inflated view of himself as compared with everyone else, and who had a succession of affairs, the most recent being with one of his employees. He's been living with her for quite a while. His wife, Dana, filed for divorce more than a year ago. Again, there are three children in this family, although only one, a girl now aged 14, is still at home. Like many girls, she loved her father very much and wanted to be loved and approved by him. She even moved in with her father, his girlfriend, and her two daughters for several months. While there, the woman's daughters invited some of their male friends over, and they raped the girl, after which she moved back to her mother's home. Jim never went after the young men who raped his daughter.

Jim is paying some child support for the daughter, but no health insurance, and he's already said that the support will cease when she turns 18. There will be no support for her college education. Due to his political connections, he has had free legal representation, whereas the litigation has already cost his wife more than $25,000— money that Dana does not have, but is endeavoring to pay off.

LLS: These are both rather bizarre cases. Even if, with your help, Sam and Dana adapt emotionally to their changed situations, they have lost a great deal in other aspects of their lives that cannot be recovered.

SDS: That's quite true, and certainly very regrettable. Equally sad is a third case. Grace is a bright woman of 49, born abroad, multilingual, and a successful businesswoman. She met and married a somewhat younger man, she put him through medical school, and they bought a home. About 2 years ago, he decided that he wanted out of the marriage, and he beat her up. Although he is now earning a very comfortable salary from his medical practice, he has not given her any money and has asserted that he wants to see her on the street as a "bag lady." Grace's lawyer, supposedly her advocate, recommended that she give her husband their home as part of a divorce settlement. The lawyer appears to have been "dealing with the enemy," as it were, rather than appropriately representing his client.

Grace, for reasons best known to her, still loves him and has been trying to save the marriage. After he announced his intention of reducing her to the homeless population, however, she became suicidal and had to be hospitalized for a time. He, meanwhile, had become involved with another, younger woman, fathered one child by her, and has another on the way.

LLS: As mental health professionals, we've all borne witness to dirty tricks and manipulations in the course of marital conflict, but these clients do seem to have more than the normal range of malice in such a situation. When you do see them, do you see just one of the parties, or the couple together, or in groups?

SDS: I usually see the couple, sometimes for protracted sessions of 2 or 3 hours, with part of the session solo for each party and then jointly. The individual sessions enable each of the spouses to say things that he or she does not want the other one to hear.

LLS: In each of the cases you've described, there is a third party involved. Is that the only cause for moving toward a divorce that you find among your clients?

SDS: No, indeed. In another case, for example, the wife was almost chronically depressed. The husband tolerated this, more or less, for years, and finally decided that he couldnt go on living this way. They came for counseling, and she made some half-hearted efforts to be a bit livelier, but couldn't maintain that behavior. In yet another case, the husband experienced a mid-life crisis, which he felt could best be resolved by making a new life for himself.

LLS: Do any of your clients come in complaining that the spouse is no longer the person "I loved and married"?

SDS: Some of them do, but the truth of the matter is that most people do change as long as they live, and what may have been common interests when they married also change as they have differing experiences. They meet different people in the course of daily life, each may develop new interests, or perhaps only one changes and the other remains rooted in an earlier stage. In addition, what may have been an attraction initially sometimes becomes an annoyance later on.

LLS: Are you thinking here of the 22-year-old who was the "life of the party" and at 52, is still telling the same jokes? Or the flirtatious or sexy young woman who is perceived 20 years later as behaving inappropriately and in a way that is threatening to her husband?

SDS: Those behaviors and others. For example, someone who is attracted to an independent thinker of 25 may, 20 years later, see that individual as perverse, selfish, or autocratic.

LLS: If you were speaking to a group of married couples, or to family counselors in training, what would be your advice to them?

SDS: First of all, I would hope that the couple would come for counseling while the marriage is still salvageable, before it gets to a crisis stage. I would suggest to the couple whose marriage seems to be going stale that they change some of their activities, develop new interests together or at least share in some of each other's interests, that they visit friends more often or take a "honeymoon" weekend where they could rediscover each other away from their normal responsibilities. One couple, for example, pretended to be secret lovers. Once a month, she would don sunglasses, meet him at an out-of-the-way restaurant where they would flirt over dinner. Then they'd check into a motel for the night. It worked!

For mid-life couples particularly, there is a need for them to support each other as they confront one form or another of the "mid-life crisis" rather than complaining to and about each other.

They also both need to make an effort to remain attractive in appearance and not let themselves go. That's true for men as well as women. These may be obvious proposals, but too often they're overlooked. Finally, the couple needs to communicate. Lack of communication is a problem in any marriage.

LLS: Sid, this has been a very interesting session, for which I thank you. I don't envy your having to try to help some of these people because their difficulty in moving forward must make counseling sessions quite painful for you. Given the nature of the cases you described, it almost seems as if someone wished a version of the ancient Chinese curse on you: "May you live in interesting times!"

■   ■   ■

6

Separation and Divorce in Mid-Life: Variations on a Theme

Lita Linzer Schwartz, PhD

What do you mean you're leaving? ... After more than 20 years of marriage! To me, marriage is for life. You know, "for better, for worse," ... *Where* am I supposed to live? ... What about our children? ... Suppose I get sick—what do I do about health insurance ... Can't we work this out? ... Won't you reconsider? ... Am I a used commodity, to be discarded like an old glove in this "throw-away" society?

If this sounds like a woman unexpectedly caught in mid-life with an imminent separation, you're right. Although surely women also leave their husbands after two or three decades of marriage, the distraught client more typically in the therapists's office is a wife whose husband has announced that he's leaving, never to return. The reasons for the departure vary, as the case illustrations to follow show, but the reaction to the impending separation and divorce, for a male or female client, is almost uniformly one of traumatic stress. (Even a mutual decision to separate after many years of marriage is traumatic. The focus here, however, is on those situations that are more unilaterally decided.)

A host of problems are created for men and women in their mid-life years who suddenly find themselves alone via rejection when they had instead anticipated perhaps a richer life in their mature years, and a leisurely, or at least a companionable, retirement with their spouse of two or more decades. Before discussing individual cases, however, let us look at some of the potential difficulties that arise for the people involved.

There may be, first of all, a severe emotional reaction for the one who is left by another, and even for some of those who decide to leave (Kaslow & Schwartz, 1987). Depression is often the diagnosis, with sleeplessness, lack of appetite and consequent loss of weight (or sometimes compensatory overeating), prolonged crying bouts, and difficulty functioning in everyday matters as key symptoms. In addition, there may be considerable loss of self-esteem, feelings of helplessness, and growing anger along with gnawing bitterness. Because several of these behaviors and feelings can be health threatening, initial treatment must be focused on helping the client to sleep, eat, and attend to daily tasks in a more constructive way.

Second, there are real financial problems to be faced. How large a "pot" is there from which husband and wife can draw economic support? Should the one who is left have to be the one who also substantially reduces his or her standard of living? As was pointed out in Weitzman's (1986) study, the impact of divorce on wives was that their incomes dropped by some 73%, whereas their husbands' incomes rose about 42% in the year following separation. Even if today's figures are somewhat reduced, the trends remain in the same directions.

In many cases, given the socialization of the 1950s when many of these mid-life couples were married, the wife may never have been employed outside the home and may have few marketable skills. Women in this age cohort "bore more children than did either their parents" or their children's generation, children who constituted the "baby-boom" generation. Because most of these women did not anticipate having careers, few of them prepared for careers (Clausen & Gilens, 1990, pp. 596–597). If the woman is in her 50s, as in two of the cases to be discussed here, and has limited or no work experience, as is true in one of these cases, her chances of being employed in a job with a decent salary (i.e., one that will permit her to live at least nearly as well as she did while married) are poor. This certainly increases both her anxiety and her depression. Even some women in their 40s have either been primarily wives and mothers, or employed in "second-income" type jobs, so that they experience similar financial crises.

Yet a third problem concerns the individual's identity, again more frequently the problem of the woman than the man. If the husband was a businessman, a professional, or an employee in a corporate structure, socially the woman was usually known as "so-and-so's wife." With the separation, she loses that identity. Does she have one of her own or can she be helped to create one?

Fourth, and also in the "social" category, is the not-so-minor matter of socializing. Although the single man is usually welcomed at parties, the single woman is more often perceived as a potential threat to others' marriages and finds her invitation calendar sharply cut. Unaccustomed to going out evenings alone, she has to develop a new attitude, a new network, and new activities if she is not to sit home bemoaning her loneliness. Actually, both men and women who have a social support network tend to make a better adjustment to their single status.

Fifth, for women in their middle years, whether 42, 52, or 62, dating is not only alien after 20 or more years of marriage, but they are rarely prepared to be the "seekers" rather than the "sought." Some are comfortable with singles' groups or singles' bars; others panic at the thought of following (or simply reject) this path. Even if they do meet a man, they wonder about how to behave, what to do if he makes physical advances, whether it's OK to have sex with him on a second or third date, whether to consider remarriage, or—Heaven help them!—what to do if the man rejects them. Men, similarly, find it difficult to date, are not sure of what the woman expects or wants of them (either physically or in terms of gender-oriented attitudes), and are equally fearful of rejection. In addition, today there is a very real concern about contracting the human immunodeficiency virus (HIV)/acquired immunodeficiency syndrome (AIDS) virus or another sexually transmitted disease, which may not be apparent until several years after infection by a casual or a frequent partner in either individual's past.

Some of the factors affecting persons experiencing divorce are shown in Figure 6.1. Certainly the presence or absence of preseparation, and the number of days or weeks since the separation occurred, will affect the client's emotional state when first seen by the therapist. Locus of control (Barnet, 1990) and level of self-esteem will help to determine the outcome of therapy. Other factors that affect both the plight and the recovery of the client can also be seen in Figure 6.1.

Three Separate(d) Women

To illuminate some of these problems, let us consider real-life clients. Three women who sought therapy presented similar problems in the sense that each had just separated from a long-term spouse, each was at some point of what's considered "middle age," and each needed or wanted help in determining new directions for her life. They were very different, however, in personality and in life experience.

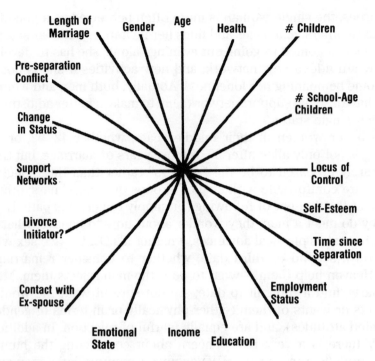

Figure 6.1.   Factors affecting the divorced.

One Who Was a "Leaver"

Bea, age 43, had been married for 20 years when she separated from her husband for the second time. (The first time was 13 years earlier, just before the birth of their son.) She had asked Bill to leave because of increasing strain over his drinking, the lack of sex in their marriage for the previous 4 or 5 years, and his insecurities. At the initial visit, she said that she still loved her husband but felt much more peaceful without him.

Bea was concerned about the effects of the separation on her children, Maria, age 17, and Ned, age 13, and felt pulled in opposite directions about whether to reconcile or to seek a divorce. Her agitation, anxiety, and depression continued for the following 3 or 4 months, during which time she lost 24 pounds. By 5 months postseparation, she was leaning toward divorce and was no longer wearing her wedding ring. She also reported that Ned didn't care whether his father ever came home again, and that Maria, although defensive of her father, felt uncomfortable when with him.

Bea's strengths included the fact that she held a responsible job as receptionist in a professional office and that she had a need to "assume control" (a trait, she said, that contributed to the marital difficulties). She also had the ability to weigh the potential positives and negatives of her options, although this sometimes kept her from making decisions. Assured that her feelings and indecision were quite normal at this stage, discussion of daily events, contacts with Bill, suggestion of previously unthought-of options, and possible consequences of her decisions took up most of the therapeutic hours. At her request, I also loaned her several books, some professional and some less so, that she found helpful (Cauhape, 1983; Charny, 1972; Kaslow & Schwartz, 1987; Lerner, 1985; Little, 1982; Shahan, 1981).

By 9 months after the separation, Bea was functioning very well in her personal life as well as on the job. She had regained some of the lost weight, was socializing with friends, had decided to take the children on a trip to celebrate her daughter's high school graduation, and planned to seek a divorce within a few months after that event. Bill was providing funds for the children as well as the house and, she thought, was living with someone. Her depression had lifted, agitation was reduced almost totally, and she was looking ahead to independent living. Socially, however, she found the dating scene bleak and had decided to create her own activities rather than go to bars or singles' groups. Almost a year after she terminated therapy, Bea sent a cheery note just to say that life was moving along smoothly. Obviously she had adapted positively to her situation, which was, after all, the goal of therapy.

Left—Again!

In complete contrast, although an incomplete case at this time, is Gloria, age 58, whose second husband left her after almost 19 years of marriage, two children, and several affairs (his). Her remarriage some 8 years later followed a difficult time raising two emotionally troubled youngsters without any financial support from their father. Her second husband, Jack, had been wheelchair-bound since a serious illness in his late teens. He had also been married before and had two grown children from his first marriage. Gloria was very caring and loving throughout their marriage, declared that she would never leave him, and could not comprehend why or how he could leave her.

Gloria and Jack were complete opposites in temperament. He, despite an almost 100% physical disability, had become an attorney, was outgoing, and enjoyed being with friends. She was very sensitive to love and rejection and, particularly after very painful injuries suffered in a accident several years earlier, was very dependent—virtually an example of "learned helplessness." It is quite evident that emotional crises exacerbate the chronic pain from which she suffers. At 58, Gloria has no real work experience and, due to recurring surgery for her injuries, is unlikely to be able to acquire training or handle any long-term job commitment.

When seen initially, Jack and Gloria had been separated for only a few weeks and had agreed to try to mediate the situation. Despite his need for physical assistance, he felt he could no longer cope with her dependence, depression, and overall negativism. She was furiously angry at this rejection, but wanted him to return. Several problems were apparent:

- Jack obviously intended to seek a divorce at some point, although he was willing at the time to provide lifetime financial support for Gloria.
- Gloria could not deal with the word *divorce* and was devastated by his move.
- There were limited funds in the common "pot" with their home as principal asset, and some decision had to be made about selling it (something else that Gloria could not deal with, even 3 months after the separation).

Although the meetings with the couple occurred early in Gloria's separation, it was apparent that she had a number of difficulties that are commonly seen: her age, which would be against her in the labor market even if she had recent work experience; her history of dependency and her sensitivity to rejection, which make it difficult for her to confront and deal with the new reality; and her chronic depression that makes a reconciliation most unlikely. (Due to a number of family losses as well as her own accident, there were legitimate reasons for adjustment disorders, but there had apparently been no positive rebound from these events.) Discussion with both Gloria and Jack suggested that he was willing to be relatively patient about long-term solutions to their situation, but that only with persistent encouragement to face reality might she be able to deal even with the short-term adjustments that were necessary. It was an achievement of sorts to have her speak with Jack civilly enough to work out current, temporary financial arrangements.

The principal therapeutic task, and it promises to be a sizable one, is to help Gloria face the present and the future with more control and less sense of being a victim than has been true for her in the past. If she continues to focus on her unhappy history, she is less likely to come out of her depression or to deal with the realities of her position. Gloria's strengths, although she doesn't recognize them as such yet, lie principally in the fact that she *has* survived a number of major crises. Supportive therapy is a must here because she is fragile and dependent, but cognitive therapy must also be used if she is to weather this crisis as she has her earlier ones and somehow become stronger in the process.

One Who Was Left

In the third instance of a woman facing a new status in mid-life, there are limited elements in common with each of the previous two clients. Judy, age 52, was informed "out of the blue" by her husband of 30 years that he was leaving her. She found out a few weeks later that not only was he leaving her for another woman, but that he had been having affairs for several years. Her initial disbelief and feelings of rejection were thus compounded with anger at the long-standing deception and abuse of marital trust that had occurred. Although Judy's feelings of self-esteem as wife and woman were understandably shaken, her status as a college professor and the respect and support of her colleagues were used as avenues to restore her self-concept as a worthwhile individual. The depression that followed her husband's announcement, which cost her sleep, about 25 pounds, ability to concentrate, and considerable anxiety, took longer to eradicate.

About a year into therapy, Judy was asked to look back and think about what factors in her life were helping her to recover, which she was doing by then. She responded that the reality testing and new ways of thinking that she had learned in therapy (a principal one being to consider what events and behaviors she could control and which she couldn't) were obviously important, but so was the fact that she had a job to do each day that required her to function as a professional. Additionally, she had the emotional support of her young adult children, members of her family of origin, and a few very close friends. There were major decisions to make about her present and future life-styles and about how to handle the impending divorce, but she also was determined not to become a bitter person, despite the anger and hurt she was experiencing.

Once she was able to concentrate on the printed word, she, like Bea, found bibliotherapy of some help in dealing with her questions and feelings in her new status. Of course, she also had anxieties about a social life and how to handle dates should any come her way, and there were many discussions of how "morality" had changed since her earlier dating years. Again, like Bea, she rejected singles' bars in favor of developing new networks and new activities.

For Judy, apart from the rejection that precipitated the divorce, there had to be a reorientation to a life that was the opposite of what she had been anticipating only a short time prior to her husband's departure. Instead of long-term planning for weekends in their vacation home and more extensive travel now that the children were grown, she had to learn to live "a day at a time" and realize that she would have to find new traveling companions or travel alone. Her feelings of vulnerability, due to living alone in the family home, driving alone at night, and occasional bouts of illness, increased markedly, but were gradually reduced as she succeeded in handling each day (and night).

Judy's strengths, with encouragement, were her will to come out of this crisis an independent and well-functioning individual, and the fact that she already had a career. From this base, she could be helped to cope with the pain of rejection by erstwhile friends as well as her ex-husband's family. She learned to make decisions in all areas of her life, sometimes aided by a few trustworthy advisors where she lacked needed information. Like Gloria, she had been "shell-shocked";

like Bea, she had the resiliency and developed the independence, through the combination of cognitive therapy and bibliotherapy, needed to make a new life.

Comment

In each of these cases, there were times when it was necessary to suggest that other professionals, such as lawyers and accountants, be consulted for their expertise, because even knowledgeable therapists should not overstep their professional bounds by presuming to give legal or financial advice. These three clients, sometimes "stuck in place" by their emotional upheaval and unable to move toward problem resolution on their own initiative, merely needed the suggestion of consultation to get things moving in terms of making financial arrangements, seeking mediation, or filing motions for divorce.

Why Therapy?

Cauhape put it well when she wrote, "Reorganizing life after mid-life divorce may demand intense effort and much trial and error" (1983, p. 17). It is easier to make the effort and to adapt to the trials and errors with therapeutic help. One of the early tasks of the therapist, however, is to assure the client that seeking help is constructive rather than something of which to be ashamed. For many individuals in their middle years (perhaps especially those at the upper end of the age range), both male and female, and particularly if they have had relatively healthy emotional lives up to that time, recognizing and accepting the need for temporary dependence on a therapist in this major life crisis is difficult in itself. There is a need to vent and deal with negative feelings, and an empathetic professional is of more help for this than even the closest family member or friend who will tire of the role of "crutch" after several weeks of depression and angry outbursts. There is a need to examine new options and new directions, and again the professional therapist should be able to offer more suggestions than the most well-intentioned family member or friend. It is also easier for the professional to wean the client from a dependent status to independent healthy functioning than it is for the family member or friend to withdraw from constant availability.

Radical life changes in mid-life are socially, if not emotionally, easier today for the clients one typically sees in marital and family counseling than they would have been in the years when these clients were newlyweds. For one thing, divorced people are not the pariahs they once were. For another, changes in divorce laws in almost all states have reduced the need to have nasty confrontations in court. Further, more of the educated women have developed professional or volunteer interests outside the home that can contribute to a positive self-concept.

There's no question that it is easier to help someone deal with mid-life divorce if the individual has a purpose in life that extends beyond the bonds and if the individual has healthy personality traits that will likely reemerge after the immediate shock creates a new normalcy. Indeed, Bursik (1991) found, in her study of newly divorced women, that "marital separation and divorce are often experienced as disequilibrating life changes, but ones that may foster ego development" (p. 305). Although one has to look at which aspects of the client's behavior contributed to the separation/divorce so that they may be modified, it seems more appropriate to do this in the context of reorganizing life for the future rather than dwelling in or on the past. Flach (1988) concluded his description of the resilient personality as one who has a focus, a commitment to life, and a philosophical framework within which personal experiences can be interpreted with meaning and hope, even when the life situation seems hopeless. Those who succeed in looking forward rather than backward often surprise themselves (and maybe even their therapists) by finding fulfillment in new activities that they might never have tried had they stayed married.

● ● ●

Today's version of "life begins at 40" tends to mean divorce, and possibly remarriage, for many. There are many legitimate concerns about the present and the future. However, given a basically healthy ego and personality, continuation of a satisfactory standard of living (by no means ensured under current laws), a good match in the therapist–client relationship, and effective therapy, it may be time for a new tag line ... "Life begins after mid-life divorce."

References

Barnet, H.S. (1990). Divorce stress and adjustment model: Locus of control and demographic predictors. *Journal of Divorce, 13*(3), 93–109.

Bursik, K. (1991). Adaptation to divorce and ego development in adult women. *Journal of Personality and Social Psychology, 60,* 300–306.

Cauhape, E. (1983). *Fresh starts: Men and women after divorce.* New York, NY: Basic Books.

Charny, I. (1972). *Marital love and hate.* New York, NY: Macmillan.

Clausen, J.A., & Gilens, M. (1990). Personality and labor force participation across the life course: A longitudinal study of women's careers. *Sociological Forum, 5,* 595–618.

Flach, F. (1988). *Resilience: Discovering a new strength at times of stress.* New York, NY: Fawcett Columbine.

Kaslow, F.W., & Schwartz, L.L. (1987). *The dynamics of divorce: A life cycle perspective.* New York, NY: Brunner/Mazel.

Lerner, H.G. (1985). *The dance of anger: A womans guide to changing the patterns of intimate relationships.* New York, NY: Harper & Row.

Little, M. (1982). *Family breakup.* San Francisco, CA: Jossey-Bass.

Shahan, L. (1981). *Living alone and liking it.* New York, NY: Warner Books.

Weitzman, L.J. (1986). *The divorce revolution: The unexpected social and economic consequences for women and children in America.* New York, NY: The Free Press.

■ ■ ■

7

Rebuilding Seminar for Mid-Life Divorce

Bruce Fisher, EdD

There have been about 2.4 million marriages and slightly less than 1.2 million divorces in the United States each year for the last few years (Bureau of Vital Statistics, personal communication, July 1992). Some have stated that because there has been a slight decrease in the number of official divorces, the divorce rate is going down. These figures ignore the large increase of people living together who end their love relationship and don't show up in the official divorce figures. The actual number of love relationships ending each year is still increasing at a significant rate.

Ending a love relationship is a major crisis in a person's life. Most people will eventually adjust to the crisis, but a group experience with emotional support can diminish the length of time it takes to adjust to this crisis. There is a need for effective but inexpensive group experiences to help transform the crisis into a creative experience. The Fisher Rebuilding Seminar was created to meet this urgent need in our society.

This seminar is one of the largest divorce recovery programs available for people who are ending a love relationship. With over 100,000 participants in the United States, Canada, Australia, and Great Britain, it has helped many people adjust to a major crisis. What takes place in the seminar? Why has it grown so large without any advertising? How does it help people to adjust and make their crisis into a creative experience?

History and Development

The seminar started as a 10-week pass–fail class in the fall of 1974 at AIMS Community College, Greeley, Colorado. From the very beginning, attempts were made to develop a program that met the needs of people ending a love relationship. A 16-item questionnaire was administered to the participants of the first six seminars asking what they thought was important to learn and discuss during the 10 weeks. Participants consistently chose "relationships" as the most important topic. Women chose sex as the second most important topic and love third. Men chose love as the second most important topic and sex third. All three of these topics became an important part of the Rebuilding Seminar.

One of the 16 items in the questionnaire was an item concerning children of divorce. It was never chosen as an important topic to discuss. When asked why it was not chosen, a male engineer stated, "I have so much pain of my own that I am not able to meet the needs of my kids until I heal myself." Because of that feedback, the topic of children of divorce has not been made part of the 10-week seminar but is offered as an all-day workshop for graduates of the seminar and their children upon completion of the 10-week seminar.

The seminar utilizes a psychoeducational model with a textbook, specific homework, and structured lesson plans for each of the 10 sessions. The original textbook was *When Your Relationship Ends* (Fisher, 1978). The textbook was similar to the author's other book, *Rebuilding When Your Relationship Ends* (Fisher, 1992). Reading the textbook provides an intellectual foundation so that emotional learning is easier and more profound. The seminar participants are asked to complete an evaluation form at the end of the 10 weeks.

The seminar emphasizes social, emotional, and psychological adjustment. Experience has shown that when these goals are reached, the legal and financial challenges facing people going through divorce are handled much more easily. Lawyers have begun to refer their clients to the seminar because it makes their job much easier. Some mediators have required that their clients attend the seminar before they will act as their clients' mediator. Psychotherapists often refer their clients because in individual therapy, they are unable to provide the adjustment and the emotional support found in the seminar.

The Fisher Divorce Adjustment Scale

The Rebuilding Seminar was the research topic for the author's doctoral dissertation. Research did not discover a personality instrument to measure adjustment to the ending of a love relationship, so the Fisher Divorce Adjustment Scale (FDAS) was developed as part of the doctoral dissertation (Fisher, 1976). The difference in the pretest, posttest gain scores between the experimental seminar and the control group using the FDAS were significant at the .05 level on the six subtests and total score. The FDAS is currently used as a pretest instrument to give participants feedback on what areas they need to work on during the 10 weeks, and as a posttest instrument to give feedback about the areas of personal growth that took place during the 10 weeks.

The FDAS is a 100-item scale with the answers being five choices ranging from "almost never" to "almost always." The alpha internal reliability for the total score is .985. The subtest scores range from .87 to .93 reliability. There have been over 100 doctoral dissertations using the FDAS.

Figure 7.1 is an FDAS research sample "Profile Sheet" showing the total score and the six subtests of self-worth, disentanglement, anger, grief, social intimacy (trust), and social self-worth. Because self-worth and grief are important areas of divorce adjustment, the FDAS emphasizes these subtests with 25 self-worth items and 24 grief items. The sample population N in this research profile is 497 participants from the Rebuilding Seminar; 75% were female and 25% were male. The participants were from 40 classes in eight states. At the bottom of the sheet are the pretest and posttest raw score points with a total gain score of 66 points. Males score lower on the FDAS pretest but show from one third to one half more gain points than females during the 10-week seminar, which results in their posttest scores being comparable to females. This research was completed in 1980.

The seminar has improved and evolved since 1980 and is a much more powerful experience today. Figure 7.2 is a class average of a recent seminar showing a total gain score of 101 points. This is a typical class gain if the facilitator has attended the Facilitator Training Workshop.

Description of the Seminar

The typical class format of this seminar is as follows. During the first 45 minutes, the participants report their experience of doing the homework in small groups with a volunteer helper leading the group. Seminar size is normally around 25 participants. The larger the group, the more need there is for small-group activities. The next activity is a large-group presentation and discussion of the

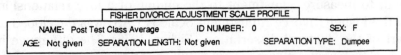

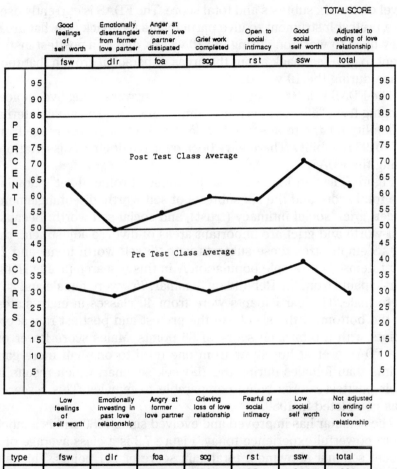

type	fsw	dlr	foa	sog	rst	ssw	total
Pre	87	77	37	82	25	31	339
Post	102	92	45	100	30	36	405

Copyright: Family Relations Learning Center, 1978, 1992

Gain 66 Points

Figure 7.1. Fisher Divorce Adjustment Scale. Research sample. © Family Relations Learning Center, 1978, 1992.

reading assignment and topic. These two activities normally complete the first 90 minutes of each session. After a break, there are normally small-group experiential activities related to the topic for that session.

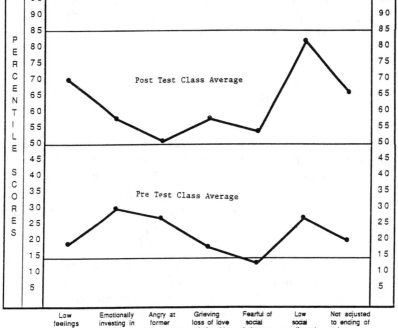

Figure 7.2. Fisher Divorce Adjustment Scale. Recent seminar example. © Family Relations Learning Center, 1978, 1992.

The seminar has been offered in many different time frames. A weekend seminar is an intensive experience, but the participants do not have enough time to do homework and integrate the learning. This results in regression after the weekend. Six-week seminars help the participants to adjust to their divorces, but do not allow enough transformation to improve future relationships. Ten weeks, with 30 contact hours, allow participants not only to adjust to their divorces but also to transform enough so that they are able to improve their future relationships either with their former love partners or with new partners. (It is estimated that about 5% of the seminar graduates return to their former love partners in an attempt to make their marriages work instead of divorcing.) The success rates of future relationships for graduates is much higher than for the general population as measured by the next relationship after the seminar lasting about 75% of the time. Divorce recovery groups meeting for less than the 30 contact hours minimize the chances of participants' transformation resulting in healthier relationships after divorce.

The Volunteer Support System

A firefighter attended the seminar in 1976 and attended every other week of the 10 weeks because of his work schedule. He returned and attended the five sessions he missed during the next 10-week seminar. His support was so helpful, especially to the women in the seminar, that he was asked to return for the next seminar as a volunteer helper. This was the beginning of the volunteer program, which has remained an important part of the seminar.

Volunteers are graduates of the seminar who are selected and asked to come back as support persons for the next seminar. They attend a 1-day Volunteer Training Workshop, which focuses on active listening skills. Ideally, there should be one volunteer helper for every five seminar participants. Volunteers lead small-group discussions, contribute to the large-group seminar activities, and support the participants outside of the class meetings with phone calls and other activities such as having lunch together. The goal is for each participant to receive at least two calls from volunteers between the first and second sessions of the seminar. If this happens, then the participants will start calling and supporting each other. By the second session of the seminar, the support system is working.

Seminar Topics

Session One: The Rebuilding Blocks

The textbook arranges the 15 stumbling blocks in the rebuilding process after a crisis into the shape of a pyramid, which symbolizes a mountain. Adjusting to a crisis is like having to climb a mountain when you don't know how to climb. The textbook provides a trail guide to help the participants climb the adjustment mountain more effectively. The opening night presentation not only helps people to obtain an overview of the adjustment process, but the feedback is predictable. "I thought I had worked through the process but hearing the presentation tells me I still have more to do" is a typical response. Session One is open and free to the public, and everyone is encouraged to attend the first half of the session.

After the break on opening night, participants introduce themselves, and the group process begins. Homework includes reading the chapter on adaptive behavior for the next week, as well as calling at least two other participants in the class in order to start building a support system. As already mentioned, the participants will seldom call others until they have been called by the volunteer helpers. The participants are discouraged from becoming emotionally and sexually involved with each other. They are greatly relieved to be free of the romantic games going on in the singles' subculture and are glad to support the no-dating rule.

Session Two: Adaptive Behavior

The topic for the second session is adaptive behavior. People going through divorce have a need to perform an autopsy on their dead relationship and discover why it died. This session helps them to do that. The majority of participants have identified their past relationships as overresponsible or underresponsible, with one person being the caregiver and the other being the taker. They also identify with other kinds of adaptive behavior in their past relationships such as being perfectionistic, pleasing people, and avoiding feelings.

When the participants were growing up, many did not feel they were getting enough love and attention. They found different ways of becoming adaptive in order to feel more loved. This childhood adaptive behavior becomes maladaptive in their adult relationships and results in polarizing. It is a specific kind of codependent relationship. The overresponsible person behavior is illustrated in the following statement: "If the person I married is not underresponsible enough, I train them to be more underresponsible." The caregiver is a good giver to others, but a poor taker. He or she needs to learn to be "responsible to self" rather than being overresponsible.

The homework assignments are designed to help people transform. An example of the homework for overresponsible people is to ask another person to do something for them, and to say no when another person asks them to do something for him or her. The perfectionist is asked to not make the bed for the next week. The intellectual, nonfeeling person, often male, is to write 10 "I feel" statements each day. If the underresponsible persons are given homework, doing it might keep them from becoming responsible for themselves. They are asked to create and implement their own homework so they can better learn how to be more responsible.

People readily see the need for the homework. Any ideas of looking for a mate in the class are greatly diminished when the person discovers how adaptive he or she has been in past relationships. The more maladaptive the person's behavior is, the more difficult it is for him or her to do the homework. The calls from the volunteer helpers often are important to help participants complete their homework, because this homework is difficult. It's hard to change old patterns of behavior.

All participants are asked to identify what feelings they feel when they do the homework. They usually feel one of these five feelings: (a) rejection, (b) guilt, (c) anger, (d) low self-worth, and (e) fear. They may also have learned adaptive behavior as a gender role behavior such as the male being the overresponsible bread winner, or the female the overresponsible family caregiver. The feelings underneath the behavior keep the person doing adaptive behavior and are related to the unmet needs in childhood. The participants are given suggestions on how to work with the feelings that keep them doing adaptive behavior in their adult relationships. They are given homework on learning to nurture themselves in order to get their emotional and social needs met that they didn't perceive were met as a child.

This is probably the most important session of all 10 sessions in helping the participants change their behavior in future relationships. This topic is discussed in the second session so the participants will have 8 more weeks to practice overcoming their adaptive behavior and learn to take charge of their lives. It appears few people change this behavior on their own without intervention of some sort. If a divorce recovery program does not help the participants deal with their adaptive behavior, they probably will repeat their maladaptive pattern of interaction in the next relationship. Not only will the new partner resemble their old partner, the new partner will often have the same first name. Group cohesiveness and emotional support in the seminar usually occurs after this session if the volunteer helpers are doing their job of being supportive to the participants.

Session Three: Grieving the Many Losses

Death has funerals and rituals that help people grieve. However, people ending a relationship through divorce often do not know they are grieving. Reading the book and the opening night presentation help them to realize they are grieving, identifies specific grief symptoms such as the inability to read and concentrate, and gives them permission to grieve as an emotionally healthy behavior. One of the items that has good statistical discrimination in the FDAS is, "I sigh a lot." A person who is grieving normally sighs a lot.

The main activity after break in this session is for participants to write a letter of good-bye to one of their losses. Participants are helped to see and understand that they are not only losing the marriage and the former love partner, but they are also losing dreams for the future, pets, the family home, friends, status, and self-worth. They are helped to see that often they have not worked through a loss from the past such as their parents' divorce, a death of a loved one, or a loss of love in childhood. The present pain may motivate them to deal with unresolved past pain. A person has the opportunity as part of the adjustment process to work through any feelings they have not worked through in the past. These feelings may not only be grief but loneliness, low self-worth, anger, and so forth. People can become "weller than well" as part of the adjustment process.

The participants usually experience a great deal of grief in the week following this seminar. It is important for the volunteer helpers to be supportive this week.

Session Four: Anger

A large percentage of people in our society do not handle anger appropriately in their relationships. Frequently, people state during this session that they never had a fight or disagreement in their marriage until the day they separated. When the participants are asked to identify what they learned from their family of origin about anger, they have difficulty listing anything positive.

Ending a love relationship encourages everyone to express all of the anger they were never able to express in the marriage. The adversarial process in the legal system has dubious value in helping people deal with anger. Quite frequently, making your former love partner the adversary helps to express the unexpressed anger, but it can leave emotional scars for both the adults and the children. Research using the FDAS indicates the average person remains angry for 3 years after the physical separation. The stumbling block of anger takes more time to work through than any of the other stumbling blocks (Fisher, 1976).

An FDAS item on anger that has good statistical discrimination is, "I blame my former love partner for the failure of my love relationship." A good indication of health is when a person is able to take ownership for anger instead of blaming the former love partner.

Small-group activities in this session include doing body sculptures developed by Virginia Satir (Satir, 1976). Placing their bodies into the different types of relationships, such as the martyr position, encourages participants to actually feel the anger. Anger is not only dissipated during this session, but ways of changing behavior such as being assertive, taking ownership for the angry feelings, and realizing the sources of anger are also taught.

Session Five: Self-Worth

The author's doctoral dissertation found that recently separated people scored at the 28th percentile on the Tennessee Self-Concept Scale (Fisher, 1976). Ending a love relationship affects feelings of self-worth. Seminar activities include writing "20 things I like about myself," and the "warm fuzzy circle" where a person on the "hot seat" has to listen and accept compliments from the other participants. The lower the person's feelings of self-worth, the hotter the hot seat is when they are receiving compliments. The participants leave this session with the greatest emotional high of any of the 10 sessions. The remaining five sessions of the seminar are usually fun and exciting after this session.

Session Six: The Shell, Rebel, and Love Stages of Growth and Development

Approximately half of the seminar participants describe their partners as going through rebellion. This is sometimes labeled the male mid-life crisis. But why do males and females of all ages go through this supposedly male mid-life crisis? It is part of a person's growth and development to individuate from the expectations of family of origin and society. It almost always ends a love relationship when one of the partners in a marriage is growing through this identity crisis.

Almost always, the partner is emotionally drained and devastated by the behavior of the partner in rebellion. The person in rebellion is often going through the process like a person lost in the woods who keeps running into trees and falling down and never gets through the process. The psychoeducational model is especially helpful for both the person in rebellion and his or her partner in dealing with this stumbling block.

One woman read in the textbook, "A person in rebellion often dumps a spouse when in reality they are trying to get rid of a person from the past" (Fisher, 1978). She called her partner whom she had asked to leave and confessed that she had dumped him when she was trying to deal with her mother. She asked him to come back, and they were able to save their marriage.

The behavior of the person in rebellion is easily identified, and people are amazed at how accurately the following describes the behavior of their partner. These characteristic behaviors are almost always present in the rebellion process. The process starts when the person begins to feel so many internal emotional pressures because he or she feels he or she always has to do the "shoulds." He or she relieves these pressures with the following behaviors.

- The person projects his or her pain by stating to the partner, "It is your fault. As soon as you change, I will be happy."
- The person starts doing what he or she wants to do instead of the shoulds, and can't understand why other people are so upset at doing what feels so good to him or her.
- The person finds another person to talk to because he or she "can't talk to the spouse anymore." This other person is often younger and of the opposite sex. The spouse and friends look upon this relationship as an affair, but the person in rebellion states it is a platonic relationship.
- The person in rebellion desires less responsibility and often changes to a less responsible job or quits working entirely. He or she is also a very underresponsible parent when in rebellion, and often looks and acts much like a teenager.
- The person in rebellion maintains he or she has to do this process alone and doesn't need to have therapy or to attend the divorce seminar.
- The person can smell a parent figure a mile away and expresses rebellion by making his or her partner a parent figure. (The partner is usually already parental and controlling. It is another adaptive behavior similar to those discussed in Session Two.)

The partner takes these six types of rebellion behavior personally, and it is no wonder he or she becomes overwhelmed and emotionally drained. Such partners need to learn to sit back and watch the show and do emotional self-care to overcome the parental behavior. If the person in rebellion is able to realize it is an internal battle between his or her "should" and "want" parts, and if the partner of the person who is in rebellion can realize he or she needs to understand and work through being parental in the relationship, the chances of the marriage lasting are greatly increased.

Session Seven: Masks

People in marriages wear a multitude of emotional masks. Examples might be the nice guy, the joker, the people pleaser, the Barbie doll, and the dependable one. People wear these masks they learned in childhood to avoid rejection and abandonment. They believe that people will like them better if they wear the mask. One of the consequences of wearing a mask is a lack of closeness and intimacy. Wearing a mask encourages the rejection and abandonment it is designed to avoid.

The seminar activity in this session is to share with others the type of mask each participant has been wearing. People feel vulnerable and afraid to share their masks and are pleasantly delighted to discover they feel emotionally close to the other seminar members when they self-disclose. This session is very helpful for people to be more open and honest in their future relationships.

Session Eight: Love

The homework given in the seventh session to prepare for this session is for participants to write a definition of love: "Love is _____ ." This is a very difficult homework assignment. Usually the participant states, "I thought I knew what love was but I guess I don't."

The emphasis in this session is self-love, or learning to love one's self. It is amazing how difficult this concept is for the participants. People in our society have learned that loving one's self is selfish. What a change it is when participants are able to feel comfortable with loving themselves.

Session Nine: Growing Relationships

Often people enter into another love relationship soon after they have ended their marriage. This is sometimes called a "rebound" relationship. When this new relationship ends, it often is more emotionally painful than when the marriage ended. The person might say, "Ending the marriage just happened, but ending another relationship is a pattern. I really need help." The pain motivates people to look at themselves, and frequently this is when they decide to participate in the Rebuilding Seminar. Maybe 20% of the participants in the seminar have had another relationship end after their divorce, and are actually adjusting to the ending of two relationships. In addition, after the class is completed, many participants will have more short-term relationships as part of their adjustment process. The need for the participants to better understand these short-term relationships is great.

Reframing is an important aspect of the seminar. Calling the relationship a "growing" relationship instead of "rebound" helps the person to gain a new perspective. Awareness that a growing relationship can be an important part of the adjustment process is helpful. The person has normally given away his or her personal power by believing he or she has found the "one and only" in the new relationship. The person believes the happiness he or she is feeling is due to the influence of the other person. The happiness might be partly due to the "honeymoon" phase of a new relationship, but the person might be developing new patterns in the relationship that are more healthy. The attempt to create a healthy relationship to help him or her work through the adjustment process can be very beneficial. The "healthy" patterns feel good even though sometimes the person ends the growing relationship because "healthy" feels uncomfortable.

Participants need to realize these growing relationships are transitional and usually do not become long-term, committed relationships. Having a lot of "future expectations" about this relationship becoming another marriage can limit the growing aspects of the relationship.

The friendships made with other participants in the seminar are healthy relationships with awareness, good communication, ownership, and commitment. These friendships often persist after the seminar is completed. It is pointed out to the participants that experiencing healthy relationships in the seminar can be the beginning of building and creating healthy relationships in the future.

Session Ten: Sexuality

This topic is fearful for many participants. It is an important topic that participants have difficulty dealing with realistically until they have worked through much of the adjustment process. There were rules and rituals in the dating game before they were married, but someone has changed the rules. It seems like there aren't any rules! It is a culture shock for many the first time they attend a singles' dance or social event. People need to face their fears and deal with this very important topic.

One activity that is helpful is to have the males and females break into separate groups and come up with a list of questions they would like to ask the opposite gender but are afraid to ask. If the participants can get beyond the many and various ways they act when uncomfortable, this exercise is tremendously helpful. Women ask men how they feel when women ask them out and offer to pay for the meal. Men ask the women if they are expected to make a pass in order for the women to feel attractive or desirable. Getting information is helpful for the participants to make more appropriate and loving decisions when they are able to enter into the dating part of the adjustment process.

Conclusion

There are some interesting evaluations concerning the value of this seminar. Absences and dropouts are few, especially if the seminar has fewer than 20 participants. People look at the seminar as the highlight of their week. The dropouts are usually those who have gone back to their old love relationships in an attempt to make them work. They state, "I am trying to make my relationship work. Why should I be taking the Divorce Seminar?"

Another criterion is the attitude of the participants about the seminar ending. During the fifth or sixth week, they will often express "separation anxiety" and wonder what they are going to do when the seminar ends. If the seminar was effective and operated as designed, at the end of 10 weeks people will leave with no regrets or feelings of needing more sessions. They will be ready to get on with their lives. However, if the seminar was not as effective as is possible, the participants will request more than the 10 sessions. If there are several wanting to repeat the seminar soon after completion, it indicates the seminar has not been as effective as possible.

The author's dissertation measured how people felt about their physical appearance with the Tennessee Self-Concept Scale. This particular subtest showed the greatest difference pretest to posttest (Fisher, 1978). A successful seminar will have pronounced differences in how the people feel about their physical appearance before and after the 10-week seminar.

Churches have offered this seminar more than other agencies, with the Roman Catholic Church offering this seminar more than all the other church denominations combined. This seminar is part of the structured program offered by Beginning Experience, an international Christian organization for the separated, widowed, and divorced. Too many singles' groups are merely putting Band-aids on people's pain. Churches that realize the need to minister to people ending a love relationship need to have implemented a balance between personal growth groups and social activities.

The Rebuilding Seminar has proven to be a positive experience for those ending a love relationship. Perhaps many more of the over 1 million people who are ending a love relationship in the United States each year need a transformation experience such as the Rebuilding Seminar.

References

Fisher, B.F. (1976). *Identifying and meeting needs of formerly married through a divorce adjustment seminar.* Unpublished doctoral dissertation, University of Northern Colorado, Greeley, CO.

Fisher, B.F. (1978). *When your relationship ends.* Boulder, CO: Family Relations Learning Center.

Fisher, B.F. (1981). *Rebuilding when your relationship ends.* San Luis Obispo, CA: Impact Publishers.

Fisher, B.F. (1992). *Rebuilding when your relationship ends* (rev. ed.). San Luis Obispo, CA: Impact Publishers.

Satir, V. (1976). *Making contact.* Millbrae, CA: Celestial Arts.

■ ■ ■

PART

LEGAL ISSUES IN
MID-LIFE DIVORCE

8

Mid-Life Divorce: A Judge's Perspective

Walter M. Schackman, BA, JD, LLM

Having presided over a busy matrimonial court in New York County for the last 7 years, I perceive a number of legal issues that are unique to people in mid-life. All of these affect the mental health of the parties, and in particular their ability to cope with the stress of divorce.

We must bear in mind the proliferation of the "no fault" divorce. Until approximately 15 years ago, most states required proof that one spouse was at fault. When divorces were more difficult to obtain, the parties may have stayed together longer, thus lessening the economic impact to some extent. Today, fault has been largely eliminated, thus making divorce much more easily obtainable. Social mores have also changed, making divorce much more common. This chapter is intended to alert those professionals engaged in family counseling to some of the legal problems their clients must deal with in these times of easy divorce.

The Dissolution of the Economic Partnership

The most common victim of mid-life divorce as seen in my courtroom is the spouse of 25 years who has not been employed outside the home or who does not have joint control over the assets of the marriage.

Although we are experiencing a transitional period where husbands are beginning to appear as the dependent spouse, in the vast majority of cases it is still the wife who is experiencing the economic problems. She has worked hard through the years caring for her children and her husband, but has not earned a paycheck in many years. The divorce revolution of the past 15 years has created some new solutions to deal with her economic problems, but some of these so-called solutions may only serve to exacerbate the situation.

A few states, led primarily by California, have retained a system called community property. In those states, every dollar that is earned and all property acquired during the marriage become the equal property of both spouses. Almost all of the remaining states have turned to a system of economic partnership called equitable distribution. Formerly, in these states, the ownership of assets went to the titled spouse after a divorce, thus often depriving the nontitled spouse a share of important assets accumulated during the marriage. This unequal division of assets was sometimes compensated for by an award of lifetime alimony to the nontitled spouse. Judges could adjust the amount of the alimony according to the wealth of the titled spouse as well as that spouse's income.

Legislators sought some new solutions, largely at the behest of women's groups, so that women would be less dependent on their husbands after divorce. We are all familiar with the statistics indicating that the spouse obligated to pay alimony fails to make the court-ordered payments in a great percentage of the cases. The preferred solution is this system of equitable distribution that has been adopted by all but a few states.

Under equitable distribution, the assets acquired during the marriage are shared by the parties. Spouses who were not working outside the home receive their share assets based on their noneconomic contributions to the family. The statutes in the various states set up criteria on which the court is to base the division of these assets. For example, in New York, the criteria include the duration of the marriage; the age and health of both parties; the loss of inheritance and pension rights; the contribution of the parties toward the acquisition of the assets, including the contributions made as a spouse, parent, wage earner, and homemaker; and the probable future financial circumstances of each party (New York State Domestic Relations Law, 1980). Some states begin with a presumption of a 50% distribution to each spouse, whereas others leave the division completely up to the courts.

An interesting sidelight to equitable distribution is an expansion of the concept of marital property. What of the spouse who has given up a career to help his or her spouse to get through medical school or to obtain a license to practice law or some other profession? New York answered that in the *O'Brien v. O'Brien* (1985) case. Mrs. O'Brien worked for 7 years to allow her husband to complete college and medical school. Within weeks after obtaining his degree, Dr. O'Brien commenced an action for divorce. The court considered his license to be marital property and awarded his wife a share of the enhanced earning capacity the license afforded.

In New York, this concept has been expanded to include other professional achievements. For example, the value of Frederica Von Stade's career as an opera singer has been held to be marital property subject to equitable distribution (*Elkus v. Elkus*, 1991). Few states have followed New York's lead largely because of the difficulty in evaluating the prospective worth of the degree or achievement. Instead, the courts have awarded expanded alimony, which at the very least softens the economic blow.

Regardless of the various theories that courts use to distribute the assets and liabilities accumulated during the marriage, their function is to dissolve the economic partnership that existed during the marriage and distribute the marital assets equitably. Nevertheless, there are particular problems that need to be recognized when the marital relationship is dissolved.

The Nonworking Spouse

The spouse who has not worked outside the home during the marriage may feel particularly vulnerable at the time of divorce. Spouses with no work experience or skills should receive a sufficient amount in equitable distribution to tide them over until they return to the workforce and earn a sufficient amount to be self-supporting. However, the probabilities are that the dependent spouse will never be able to become self-supporting and thus may need to be supported for the rest of his or her life. The issue then is whether the court will order lifetime alimony, currently called maintenance. The trial courts have been cognizant of the reality that it is extremely difficult, if not impossible, for a woman over 50, with limited job skills and no recent work experience, to become self-supporting.

In my court, a husband recently presented evidence through an expert in career guidance that a 59-year-old nonworking spouse could return to the workforce after 35 years and earn approximately $19,000 per year. I rejected that testimony. Fortunately for some dependent spouses in New York, the appellate courts have recently been sympathetic and granted lifetime maintenance to spouses as young as 45 on the grounds that durational limitations should be imposed only to enable a dependent spouse to become financially independent or to allow such a spouse to restore his or her earning power to a previous level (*Brownstein v. Brownstein,* 1990). This could include rehabilitative maintenance to enable the spouse to return to school or to receive vocational training. Maintenance could also be staggered to reduce it as the spouse returns to the workforce and earns more income. Sometimes a middle-aged spouse who worked during the marriage may nevertheless be awarded lifetime maintenance when it is shown that his or her field of employment is presently depressed and unlikely to afford him or her the opportunity to be compensated at the level enjoyed during the marriage (*Zelnick v. Zelnick,* 1991).

The Abandoned Spouse

We have been considering the spouse of middle years, usually the wife, who has been fortunate enough to have a spouse who can support her or who has received a substantial award of accumulated marital property in recognition of her noneconomic contributions to the marriage partnership. What about the wife who is completely abandoned or substantially abandoned by her husband? She may be left with children who are in college or young adults who need some financial support even though the parental obligation to pay child support terminated when they reached age 21. She has insufficient income to support herself and no in-laws to help her.

This is a situation that faces countless numbers of women today whether their backgrounds are middle class or working class. It has been my observation that the working-class wives are probably more capable of surviving because they may have maintained some emotional and financial independence as a result of part-time or full-time employment. However, the middle-class wives who were in long-term marriages and devoted themselves almost exclusively to their husbands' emotional needs and to their professional and/ or social life now are without economic resources and may have few emotional resources with which to cope.

When looking for emotional or economic assistance, these women realize that their parents, if alive, are frequently elderly and need their children, rather than the reverse. Their adult children are too busy and not financially capable of lending a hand. Their lawyers do not want to see them because they don't have funds for retainers, and, even if they locate the husbands and acquire jurisdiction over them, it is very difficult to obtain money from them. Frequently, the husbands have started new families. Sometimes *pro bono* lawyers are available for these women, but the success rate in fully recovering arrears owed is low. The uniform laws recently enacted by many states to enforce child support awards do not help these older wives. It is a rare person who does not need emotional support under these circumstances.

Health Insurance

A practical and extremely important problem that can occur in mid-life divorce is the loss of health insurance. A dependent spouse can look to the Consolidated Omnibus Budget Reconciliation Act (COBRA—a federal requirement that the employer carry the spouse for a short time), but after that, difficulties arise. In mid-life, there is more need than ever for this type of protection, and I frequently find that it is almost impossible to obtain. Although this is really an economic problem, from the point of view of the therapist it is another cause of anxiety that really can be alleviated only by a practical solution, that is, obtaining coverage.

The Marital Home

This again is more often a problem for the dependent wife, but can be difficult for the husband as well. The parties have lived in a house or apartment for many years. It has become more than brick and mortar, and now they must dispose of it. Most often, the economics of a situation will prevent it from being retained by one of the parties. A trade-off can occur whereby a spouse can remain in the home by giving up some share of equitable distribution of another asset, frequently the other spouse's pension. This trade-off cannot be managed often enough. The loss of so many things by the divorce is followed by the last straw, the loss of roots, the anchor. This can occur in any divorce, but is most devastating in a mid-life separation where the parties have enjoyed many years of living in a particular place and style.

● ● ●

The specific problems to which I referred that can occur when people in mid-life are divorced are largely economic. The loss of family, companionship, love, and sense of purpose in maintaining a home for a spouse obviously must be dealt with by the mental health professional. The court can attempt to soften the economic blow, but there is often little we can do with the parties' limited resources. The old adage that "two can live as cheaply as one" is just not true.

We see in case after case the economic strain when two households are created. Often the chief provider is remarried and takes on additional responsibility. How frequently we see the middle-aged husband shed his wife of many years, marry a younger woman, and proceed to create a second family. This is not just a television script because too often it is reality. The emotional strain in both former spouses must often be ameliorated by counseling.

The role of the mental health professional in aiding the parties to overcome the effects of mid-life divorce is of paramount importance. The parties must be assisted to get on with their lives, put aside the baggage of the past, and find ways to deal with the reality of the present.

References

Brownstein v. Brownstein, 167 AD2d 127; 561 NYS2d 216 (N.Y. App. Div. 1st Dept. 1990).

Elkus v. Elkus, 169 AD2d 134 (N.Y. App. Div., 1st Dept. 1991).

New York State Domestic Relations Law, Section 236 B5. 1980.

O'Brien v. O'Brien, 66 NY2d 576 (N.Y. Ct. of Appeals 1985).

Zelnick v. Zelnick, 169 AD2d 317; 573 NYS2d 261 (N.Y. App. Div. 1st Dept. 1991).

■ ■ ■

9

Mediation and the Mid-Life Divorce

Peter D. Rogers, PhD
Martina Reaves, JD

Divorce is a difficult and stressful process at any stage of life, but the "mid-life" divorce has uniquely painful aspects—a long-term commitment with shared dreams and responsibilities, intertwined lives, a history of struggle, and the joys and sorrows of raising children. In mid-life, a divorce is not simply an event, but a collage of experiences and feelings.

The issues involved in such a divorce necessarily vary from couple to couple. Relevant variables include the length of marriage, the reasons for the divorce, the couple's work history, and their ages and economic standing. The factors seem endless. Our presentation of the issues involved in a mid-life divorce is based on more than 30 years of cumulative experience as a therapist and an attorney, often working as a team, helping lower middle to upper class couples mediate their marital dissolution.

When children are involved, the legal and emotional issues for the family "in transition" are complex. The ongoing relationships between each parent and the children will have to be worked out. In addition, after a lengthy marriage, the middle or upper class couple usually has considerable assets: a home, pension plans, investments, household items and *objets d'art*, vehicles, and so forth. These items need to be divided equitably between the parties. Because many of them have an emotional charge, the process is more difficult than an apparently simple exercise in mathematics. In reality, the couple is dissolving not only an emotional partnership, but a financial one as well.

Mediation

Couples divorcing have a variety of options available to handle their divorce. The traditional method is one in which each party has an attorney, and the two attorneys negotiate on behalf of their clients. If the attorneys cannot reach a settlement, then the issues are usually determined by a judge.

In recent years, mediation has increasingly become a preferred alternative to the traditional method. In fact, divorce mediation was hailed by Warren Burger, former Chief Justice of the U.S. Supreme Court, as the "brave new world" of settling marital disputes.

In mediation, the separating spouses agree to work with a neutral mediator (or mediation team) to resolve the issues of the division of property, custody , and support. It is important to remember that in divorce mediation, the *couple* is the client, not the husband or wife as individuals.

The mediation setting provides a safe forum in which cooperative and creative solutions may develop. It allows for the exploration of options and alternatives that might not be possible to achieve in court, where the only reference point is the law. In the process of working out an equitable agreement, many couples may learn how to cooperate in their mutual interest and avoid past mistakes.

When appropriate, mediation offers many advantages to the divorcing couple. Normally, a mediated divorce costs a small fraction of the amount required for a litigated divorce. In addition, there are often reduced emotional costs because the mediation focuses on solutions that meet the needs of both partners. A mediated divorce also lays the groundwork for the cooperation helpful to successful co-parenting. Finally, the couple is more likely to follow their agreement if each has participated in the process to reach the agreement.

Most mediations begin with an assessment session to determine whether mediation is a suitable method for the couple. In order for mediation to be successful, the couple must be able to agree to full disclosure regarding all the assets and financial issues. It is also helpful if the partners have shared goals—for example, mutual concern for the children, a wish to preserve a friendship, and a need to make their own decisions regarding the division of assets. Finally, each spouse must be able to present his or her point of view in the process.

There are a variety of mediation styles that have evolved over the past 20 years. Some mediations focus primarily on the law as the reference point for making decisions. Others use the law as only one of many reference points, with the couple choosing how much emphasis to place on what might happen in court. Sometimes mediations are conducted by teams of mediators that, in the divorce context, will often include both an attorney and a therapist. Some mediators will *only* meet with both spouses present, whereas others are willing to meet with the individuals separately.

During the process, the couple is usually asked to complete information forms about assets and debts, and to make budget projections for running their separate households. The couple is encouraged to have neutral, independent appraisals of the home, a business, automobiles, or other assets, in order for both to be fully informed on the financial issues.

When the couple reaches an agreement satisfactory to both, a Marital Settlement Agreement or memorandum of understanding is prepared by the mediator, which the couple may review with their separate attorneys prior to signing. The beauty of mediation is that the couple can make their own choices and decisions about the important matters affecting the rest of their lives.

Effects on Children

The effects of the divorce on children vary greatly depending on their ages and other factors. If the children are still minors, the parents will need to continue dealing with one another in order to co-parent. In many areas of the country, it is still the assumption that the children will live with their mother, and "visit" with their father. However, even this form of co-parenting requires organization, agreement, and a certain amount of contact between the parents to make it work.

In recent years, as more and more fathers have taken an active role in the rearing of their children, the issues of custody have become more complex. How much time will the children spend with each parent? Where will the children go to school? How will vacations be spent? Who will handle the medical care and make dental appointments? What extracurricular activities will they have, and who will pay for them? Who will provide transportation?

Frequently, a divorce will cause fathers to reevaluate their relationships with their children. No longer satisfied with the role of "bread winner," many postdivorce fathers may find that they want to increase their involvement with their children. Some children are surprised to find that they are actually getting more quality time with their fathers than ever before. Nevertheless, the sad truth is that many fathers will lose their connections with their children and become nothing more than "visitors."

Where the nuclear family has been tumultuous and chaotic, a divorce that brings an end to family conflict may be seen as a relatively positive outcome for the children. Nevertheless, younger children are apt to be self-blaming and vulnerable to gross distortions in their perceptions of their parents' emotions and needs. At this early stage of cognitive development, they are also more likely to have unrealistic hopes for parental reconciliation and fears of total abandonment.

Adolescents experience more initial pain and anger than younger children. Some adolescents become acutely anxious when they perceive how vulnerable (i.e., human) their parents really are. But for the most part, older children are able to contain the problematic aspects, despite the early disruptive effects of divorce. By using "extended family" resources such as school and peers, they are able, to a degree, to soften the effects of family stress. After the trauma of divorce is over, they are more able to resolve loyalty conflicts and accurately assess responsibility for the divorce. They may tend to withdraw from family issues and find comfort from their peers or dive into school activities.

Little or no research has been reported on the effects of divorce on college-aged or late adolescent children. In the well-known Wallerstein and Kelly (1980) sample, only 14% were defined as adolescents. However, Hodges (1986) reported a study by Bales in which 39 University of Pennsylvania college students were interviewed following the divorce of their parents. A majority reported depression, increased stress, and a sense of insecurity.

Slater, Stewart, and Linn (1983) looked at data from 217 adolescents. Remarkably, they found that boys from divorced homes had better "self-concepts" than boys from intact homes. The girls, however, had opposite findings. Generally, boys had a relatively positive view of the divorced home environment, and the girls tended to have a relatively negative view.

Two of several young women interviewed by the authors recently denied that the divorce had an effect on their current relationships, but both admitted that they were looking for "someone to take care of me." Alice is always looking for the "right guy," a man with whom she can feel "safe," someone whom she can trust. She says that she "doesn't want to be alone again." Lori said, "I still want to be a parent, but a different kind of parent. I want to provide my children with an intact family unit."

Evelyn was just preparing to enter college when her parents separated and her whole support system vanished. Five years after the divorce, she reported that she had felt abandoned by the family at the time of separation. She couldn't leave home because, all of a sudden, "home" was gone. She felt that she had to grow up very quickly, and that her parents, who had previously been available and supportive, were now too involved in their own problems to provide for her needs. She therefore threw herself into schoolwork and sorority activities, which insulated her and made her less dependent on the family.

Beth, 16 years old at the time of marital separation, felt like "the ground gave way under me." Her distress was exacerbated by the fact that she felt obligated to take care of her mother, who was a "basket case." Even though her father left, she reports not feeling abandoned because she is able to maintain frequent contact with him. On the other hand, she feels that she lost a part of her innocent childhood.

Children whose parents divorced during their adolescence are more likely to consider divorce as an option for themselves in later life. They are less likely to remain stuck in an unhappy marriage. For example, Evelyn, when asked, "What have you learned from all this...?" responded by saying, "If things get really bad, its OK to split. Divorce doesn't have to be messy."

This view is to some extent validated by a recent investigation done by Abelsohn and Saayman (1991). Studying a sample of 45 adolescents during the first 18 months of parental separation, they failed to find the expected "disastrous" results. Instead, they concluded that the mid-life divorce "... is probably within the realm of adaptation for many families and adolescents," and suggested that future research be "... less preoccupied with the risks of divorce and [focus on] the complex processes of internal reorganization in the family unit" (p. 190).

Issues Involving the Division of Property and Support

The Family Home

In many divorces, a critical issue, both legally and emotionally, is the disposition of the family home. Often, the parties have lived in the home for a long period of time, and there are significant attachments to it, the neighbors, and the neighborhood. Loss of both the marriage and the home can be devastating to many couples and their children.

Sometimes, one parent and the children are able to stay in the home because there are enough other assets to award to the other spouse. In some cases, the other spouse is willing (or court ordered) to co-own the home for a period of time for the children's benefit.

In many cases, however, the home must be sold, and the proceeds divided in some manner, which may (or may not) enable both parties to purchase a new residence. In the San Francisco Bay Area, the cost of housing is now so high that many middle-class couples are unable to repurchase homes, or even condominiums. In cases where they each manage to buy, their new households are run on very tight budgets.

Medical Issues

At mid-life, some individuals find that they have medical problems that make them uninsurable. Often, the couple and their children have been medically insured through the employment of the husband or wife. However, once the divorce is final, the former spouse can no longer be covered under the employed spouse's plan. Although there are federal laws that allow the nonemployee spouse to convert to an individual policy for a certain period of time, the costs may be quite high.

The solutions to this issue vary from couple to couple. It is important that the couple be aware of the problem and look into their options prior to reaching a final financial agreement.

Child and Spousal Support/Alimony

After separation, most couples are faced with the significant economic problem of having to support two households. Often, they were barely able to make ends meet supporting one household prior to separation. Frequently, there is a sudden decrease in the standard of living for both households, although in the long run the economic effects of a lowered standard of living generally hit women and children the hardest.

The legal issues in connection with the amount and duration for the payment of child and spousal support vary from state to state. In California, for instance, child support is legally payable only until a child is 18 or 19 if he or she is in high school and living with a parent. Attempts to change the law to deal with parental responsibility for payment of college expenses have, so far, failed.

Spousal support, or alimony, laws also vary from state to state. In California, the statutes (and the laws that have been established by cases interpreting the statutes) are complex. For many couples, however, this issue of the amount and duration of spousal support goes to the heart of their marriage and divorce. It brings up issues of self-worth, who is "leaving" whom, what agreements the parties had during marriage, and each individual's sense of fairness.

It is impossible to discuss the mid-life divorce and support issues without looking at the role of gender. The stereotype of the middle-aged man leaving the marriage for another, often younger, woman is too familiar to be ignored. If the wife has not worked outside the home, or has only worked part time or sporadically, the impact of the divorce can be dramatic, both emotionally and financially. In many states, even if she receives spousal support, the wife may be looking at a legal system that demands or "encourages" her to become self-supporting. For women who have been in "traditional marriages" in which they have been seduced into believing the myth of lifetime security, the fear can be overwhelming. A divorce for such a woman often means returning to the workplace, with its built-in, discriminatory wage gap.

Some women seek vocational counseling to explore their options in the job market. Some return to school or obtain other training to learn a marketable skill. However, the economic reality of the job market is that women in general earn substantially less than men. In addition, a late entry into the job market often has a direct effect on the economic future of mid-life women who may be entering it for the first time.

On the other hand, the husband is often looking at the possibility of having to pay spousal support for many years. Having an end in sight to the spousal support obligation is one of the most critical desires expressed by many men at the beginning of the divorce process. This is particularly true in marriages in which the wife wants the divorce because she has "outgrown" the marriage. For these men, the thought of having to be financially responsible for many years feels grossly unfair and frightening. Many will negotiate to receive less of the property in return for an end to their spousal support obligation.

In cases in which the husband is self-employed, this issue of support becomes more difficult. In many states, including California, the business is considered a community property or joint asset, which is valued and divided along with other assets. Sometimes, the appraised value of the business in the divorce context is more than the husband would ever receive if he sold or left the business. Many men in this situation are unhappy with a system that values the business, and then orders the husband to pay a large portion of his income from the business as support for years to come.

Because of the many factors that affect the amount and duration of spousal support, resolving the issue in a mid-life divorce is often one of the most complex issues, both legally and emotionally.

● ● ●

At mid-life, a divorcing couple is faced with dissolving both a personal relationship as well as a business relationship. A multitude of decisions must be made about the children, the family home, retirement, career, the division of assets, and the payment of debts. In reality, a new plan for the future must be made by two people who had previously planned for a future together. In choosing mediation as a method to resolve these issues, each spouse is making the choice to be actively involved in planning for this future. The process may be emotionally difficult at times, but the results—both short and long term—can be worth it.

References

Abelsohn, D., & Saayman, G.S. (1991). Adolescent adjustment to parental divorce: An investigation from the perspective of basic dimensions of structural family therapy theory. *Family Process, 30(2)*, 177–191.

Hodges, W.F. (1986). *Interventions for children of divorce: Custody, access, and psychotherapy.* New York, NY: Wiley.

Slater, E.J., Stewart, K.J., & Linn, M.W. (1983). The effects of family disruption on adolescent males and females. *Adolescence, 18*, 931–942.

Wallerstein, J.S., & Kelly, J.B. (1980). *Surviving the breakup: How children and parents cope with divorce.* New York, NY: Basics Books.

Suggested Readings

Kalter, N. (1990). *Growing up with divorce.* New York, NY: Free Press.

McKay, M., Rogers, P.D., Blades, J., & Gosse, R. (1984). *The divorce book.* Oakland, CA: New Harbinger Publications.

McKay, M., Rogers, P.D., & McKay, J. (1989). *When anger hurts: Quieting the storm within.* Oakland, CA: New Harbinger Publications.

Nadelson, D., & Polonsky, D. (Eds.). (1984). *Marriage and divorce: A contemporary perspective.* New York, NY: Guilford Press.

Wallerstein, J.S., & Blakeslee, S. (1989). *Second chances: Men, women, and children, a decade after divorce.* New York, NY: Ticknor & Fields.

Weitzman, L.J. (1985). *The divorce revolution: The unexpected social and economic consequences for women and children.* New York, NY: Free Press/Macmillan.

■ ■ ■